A Smile in the Mind's Eye

A Smile in the Mind's Eye

LAWRENCE DURRELL

WILDWOOD HOUSE LONDON

First published in Great Britain 1980

Wildwood House Ltd
1 Prince of Wales Passage
117 Hampstead Road
London NW1 3EE

ISBN 0 7045 3045 7

Typeset by Red Lion Setters, London
Printed and bound in Great Britain by
Redwood Burn Limited
Trowbridge & Esher

*Dedicated to Chantal De Legume
wherever and whoever she might be?.*

I

I have been meaning to write a short account of my meeting with Jolan
Chang, a Chinese scholar and – as he would have it – gerontologist, for
some considerable time, though it has not been easy to assemble all the
impressions he left behind him after his first short visit to my Provençal
home. The word *Taoism*, for example, has always had a dramatic appeal
for me, though apart from the great poem associated with it, its Bible, so to
speak, I know but little of the Taoists and their beliefs. But ever since I fell
upon that beautiful and concise work, the *Tao Te Ching*, which contains
an enigmatic description of the great motor of the universe and its work-
ings, I felt somehow that that is what I myself believed in – or would
believe in for choice if one day I found that belief were absolutely necessary
to me.

But here I should hesitate for a moment – for what do I mean by
'belief'? The word is not to be airily tossed away in this cavalier fashion,
without some attempt to come to intellectual grips with it. In my own case
I find that with every kind of belief one must exercise a certain caution –
for it hardens into dogma if it becomes absolute rather than provisional.
The word Tao, on the other hand, suggests to me different stances (all
truth being relative) – a state of total *disponibilité*, total availability, a total
and comprehensive and wholehearted awareness of that instant where certainty breaks surface like a hooked fish. Only at this point is the spirit fully
tuned in to the great metaphor of the world as TAO. Reality is then prime,
independent of the hampering conceptual apparatus of conscious thought.
It is the flashpoint where the mind joins itself to the nature of all created
things. That poetry is Tao.

When did I first begin to harbour such ideas? It is long ago now – it must
have been during my twenty-third year, perhaps in the island of Corfu. I
cannot recall the circumstances at all clearly. I felt then that in this book I

had stumbled upon a Chinese Heraclitus, and that despite the apparent enigmas with which the poem deals, the whole thing made immediate sense to me – somewhat transcendental sense, to be sure, but absolute sense. I found it to be a creation in the same key as that of the early Greek philosophers I was then discovering. And so, diving for cherries we had thrown on the sand sea-floor of the little shrine to St Arsenius, I repeated to myself fragments of the two texts as if they had been by the same man. Of course I see now that they were – though Heraclitus's text is more fragmented than that of the Chinese sage . . . But quite apart from all this I had never in my life met any individual Chinese to talk to – and certainly never any scholar who could promise at once to explain and discuss Taoism as a living belief – which is what Chang did when he first telephoned to me in his excellent and graphic English. There was nothing in it, he added mischievously – a Taoist joke! It came about like this. For some weeks in 1976 I had been receiving letters from this unknown Chinese scholar couched in very good English from the city of Stockholm where he appeared to reside. The Taoist-gerontologist nexus became slowly clear to me when I remembered that the Taoists were absolutely obsessed by the question of immortality in this life – not in an afterworld; and their whole practice was devoted to trying to achieve this desirable state in this life, before striking out for the nirvana of the orthodox Buddhists – though of course Taoism is part of Mahayana Buddhism. But my scholar was rather a puzzle at first. He wrote in a small neat hand on several different sorts of headed paper obviously pinched from yacht clubs and hotels. I shared this magpie habit myself and perfectly understood. But he covered the whole surface of the paper with his fine script. He said that he wished to consult me about a work of scholarship he had completed, and which was already being set up for publication – and the reason he gave was that he had seen somewhere an interview in which I expressed my sympathy for Taoism.

I was of course flattered and startled, and hastened to disclaim any special knowledge of the subject. No matter, he insisted, and went on to ask if he might visit me in Provence. And no sooner had I agreed than I found him at the other end of a telephone calling me from Stockholm and proposing to reach my little local station of Lunel by dawn on the following day. It was very swift thinking and I was puzzled at the speed of the decision and the expertise over the timetables – but I was to find out that Jolan Chang was a sort of walking abacus, and that his travelling was based most strictly upon the principles of Chuang Tzu (in whose text the traveller always passes invisibly, raising no dust by his silent passage). I did not regard this admonition very literally until I met Chang and realized that if one did not live with total economy in every field one was literally prejudicing one's immortality! I thought he was simply a little miserly at first, until I twigged the immortality principle behind his tremendous frugality! In the Taoist principle there should be nothing left over when you die and 'go into the round' – not a crumb, not an undrawn breath. Taoism engenders a clean sweep. Everything must be refunded into the happy silence of the Tao!

Rising early has never been a problem; at five-thirty I lit up the dark garden and warmed the motor of the car. The owls which inhabit the old tower by the pool came whistling and skirmishing down into the lighted foliage, friendly as gun-dogs. Indeed, so often the younger ones overshoot and crash into the coloured panes of the lighted verandah, as the children used to call it. Dawn was not far off, there was a faint suspicion of darkness lifting in the east, beyond the bony *garrigues*. My little local station is quite close – about a dozen kilometres only. I have always revelled in this solitary drive to meet the early train along roads almost deserted save for the occasional lorry. The gloomy little station would be still asleep when I got there – the guard and the ticket-collector always appear like jack-in-the-boxes from nowhere, just a few moments before the bell tingles to announce the arrival of the Paris express. I was curious about Chang – what sort of man had I come to meet? I pictured someone extremely fragile and venerable and old...

The Paris 'Rapide' was punctual as always; she slid into the station pulling the long black new-look coaches. There was a Chinese youth standing at the open door of a carriage waiting for the speed to slacken. As he stepped down the ladder I took him to be about eighteen, so supple and light were his movements. He smiled and waved – I was the only person on the platform – and then leaped to the *quai* as light as a cat. Yes, it was Chang all right! It was a little while before I found out that this slim Chinese youth was around sixty years of age!

His only baggage appeared to be a couple of Air France zip-bags such as one buys in airports. He wore a light overcoat, a heavy pullover and a ski bonnet. He had sat up all night – or rather had slept sitting – to save expense and also to do a little work. The text he had brought with him looked a somewhat bulky one. But he was as fresh as a daisy, and seemed to revel in the landscapes we were soon crossing, warmed as they were by the light of the rising sun. It was a choice dawn, the countryside was fresh after a light dew, and the promise of a warm day put us both in a good humour. In the case of Chang it was also his first visit to Provence and his eager darting eye flashed about like a dragon-fly, taking everything in with an effortless zeal which made me feel that he was busy repainting it all in water-colour – transforming it in his mind into a Chinese version of Provence.

The roads were just waking up by the time we reached the village and my guest expressed his admiration for it. It is, I suppose, the most beautiful in the Languedoc, with its girdle of medieval walls and ravelins and its tumpy Roman bridge across the green Vidourle – a river which often leaps out of its bed and floods the town for an hour or two before sliding away down towards Lunel and the sea. My abandoned garden with its tall trees and hidden pool also met with his approval. Chang seemed to take in everything with a sort of panoramic vision, like a praying mantis. He gave quick little nods, as if of recognition. He did not speak any French.

My solid and sometimes rather brusque part-time maid was startled – she was already at work on the washing-up – when I walked into the kitchen with a Chinaman. He greeted her in English and then sat down quietly at the kitchen table to wait for breakfast. But here was a brief check – for he had brought his own with him, and seemed rather afraid to be subjected to anything heavier than fruit. He spoke with some diffidence, yet he had an air of great distinction about him. In fact he had the magnificent looks of a tiny Emperor as he sat at the kitchen table with a kind of regal passivity, almost a helplessness like that of hieratic personages of rank whose every gesture is studied. It was an illusion of course. He was extremely small-boned and fine in physique – he had, I discovered, pared himself down relentlessly by the diet he followed. His air of courteous authority came perhaps from the fact that he didn't fidget, he simply and happily sat, as sometimes a child will. We proposed several sorts of breakfast to him but he found the suggestions superfluous. From his little zip-bag he produced an orange and a small silver pocket knife. He crossed to the sink with the deftness of a cheetah and washed the fruit thoroughly before cutting it into quarters which he then ate slowly and with circumspection, rind and all. Meanwhile I had come to my senses and produced honey and milk and bread, and other fruit – a sort of yogi breakfast which met with his approval. He was to stay with me for a long weekend, this had been agreed; I hoped that there would be enough time, not only for the textual work, but also to enable me to show him a little of the Languedoc. For a while we sat in quiet affability, watching the maid get through her routine – she only spares me an hour a day, which is just enough to maintain the balance of things in the bat-haunted old Provençal house I inhabit, more often than not alone.

Soon she went, and it was the beginning of a marvellous long weekend – momentous for me, for it combined all sorts of choice information, a fascinating text, Chinese cooking, and – this somewhat to my surprise – a great deal of laughter. He rode life with a very light rein, my Taoist friend. Moreover it was a delightful thing – all men feel this – to spend some time locked up with a member of your own sex; in the Alps, say, or under snow, or on a windy Greek island. Here in Sommières we could make fires, experiment with cooking, quarrel, play cards, read and talk about women; nor do I think this sort of appreciation is exclusively male – women also enjoy it, the freedom from the partiality of the opposite sex. My wife used to spend a fortnight a year in a chalet in the Alps with three girlfriends, freed from the boredom of crimping male company – free to ski, quarrel, cook, read, play cards, and . . . talk about men. It is absolutely logical. So that when the maid took herself off – and she does not come on weekends – I rejoiced to find myself mewed up with a new friend who would soon turn out, I hoped, to be a storehouse of exotic knowledge, and the verifier of many an intuition I had once had in reading Chinese classics, though unfortunately always in translation.

Well, while the maid finished up, Chang elected to have a hot bath and spruce himself up after the fatigue of the long journey; I also felt that after a considered and circumspect period of smelling out his new surroundings like an animal, he had suddenly relaxed and felt himself at home. 'If you are going to cook for me, as you promised,' I said, 'it will have to be this evening because the maid, without waiting for orders, has made us a lunch – an *escalope* and a glass of wine and some rice.' He rather demurred at the mention of meat but at once added, 'I am not a fanatic, you know. Just to prove it I will have a tiny piece, and even a sip of wine.' It was a splendid bit of good manners, and while he joked about cholesterol and grease I realized that he was serious.

But how he carried all that he did in his two little satchels was a puzzle because, apart from his food (three apples, a carton of milk, some honey, nuts, and several packs of assorted vitamins) he also had a change of trousers and another pullover, as well as a dressing-gown and other sundries. I began to see him in the light of a Chinese conjurer perhaps, simply making things vanish into the little bags. He spent a long time enjoying the water and cleaning up his clothes, brushing them scrupulously and removing stains with a damp cloth. But though he proclaimed himself much restored by the bath I could see little trace of a change – he had shown no fatigue in the first place. 'The sun is shining,' he said. 'How about a walk?'

It was a good idea. He wanted to see the little medieval town and to get the feeling of his whereabouts – he was excited to be in Provence for a while. He smelt the vivacity in the French air, he said, looking about him like a precious insect.

What was more engaging still was that there was the usual Saturday market-day display laid out, bright as a bed of flowers, in the arcaded Place du Marché. This was a piece of local colour which had my friends in raptures – indeed with the vivid awnings of the *forains* and the banks of brilliant vegetables and fruit on the stalls the sight is delightful in all its sunny variety. And vegetables! Chang practically did a two-step with joy as we loitered down the great stone staircase into the little square, going slowly in order to take in the beauty of the scene. He would, he said, shop there and then for the evening; and as good as his word, he began a microscopic investigation of the vegetables on display, with the single-mindedness of a bird of prey – a keen shopper's attitude which won the instant admiration of all the village vendors for whose benefit I translated his questions. Furthermore his purchases when he made them were of a most modest kind – I did not see how two fully grown men could exist on this meagre handful of stuff which he loaded with care and love into a string bag. I said as much but he only smiled; and indeed when the time came I was astonished to find that living in his way there always seemed more than enough to eat of the delicious light fare. But when he took over the entire cuisine, allocating to me simply the task of cutter-up, we ate about five times a day – ate when we felt like it. Each meal was different, each a sort of hot snack.

* * *

So we returned triumphantly to the house to despatch our French lunch and to make preparations for the cooking of the evening meal. Chang looked over my display of knives and found them wanting. Indeed, some of them would not cut at all, and then, where, he asked, was there a suitable cutting-board? At last I found him a slice of olive-wood which he thought might do and the best of the knives, and he fell to work to clean and pare his vegetables exercising the utmost economy, using every scrap of leaf and rind. I realized then that, as he said, anything and everything is eatable if cut up in sufficiently tiny quantities. He gave me part of his loot and showed me how to operate on it, talking the while rather gravely about how Chinese cooking takes the simplest way round things. Even the teeth are spared hard use because the food is so finely chopped, while compared to all the western kitchen lumber that we use – knives, forks, and so on – the Chinaman has only two expendable sticks for his chop and one small bowl. One knife that is sharp and a cutting-board are all that is really necessary. I guiltily swore to have all my knives resharpened at the earliest opportunity. This deft and youthful Chinese presence brought a touch of exoticism to the kitchen, and I promised myself a few days full of discussion and self-cultivation – as the Taoists would have it!

But first to our muttons. Chang spread out his fat typescript upon the table for me to read at my leisure. But to begin with he proposed to fill in the background to the work of compilation he had brought to bed. I should add here that by now I had found that Chang, despite his Canadian nationality and perfect English, was not (what I had feared when I heard him on the telephone) a Chinaman born abroad; he was a homegrown specimen of the contemporary China, who had borne arms against the Japanese. He had been brought up and educated in China. He was, there-fore, thoroughly representative of Chinese culture of today, while, like all cultivated men, he was soaked in the poetry and history of China's long and variegated classical past.

He seemed somewhat anxious to underline the fact that though vege-tarian and teetotal himself it was by deliberate personal choice and not in obedience to some abstruse conviction; busily dicing up his load of vege-tables, he explained that there was in reality no such thing as a generalized diet which suited everyone. Diet was an individual affair and if one were a serious person – serious about one's mind and body and their part in the general ground-plan of the universe as a whole – then one was in honour bound to experiment and establish a suitable individual diet of one's own. He himself had only realized this relatively recently; on his arrival in Canada from China he had fallen in with the eating habits of his adopted country with disastrous results. He had become so out of condition that he was hardly able to walk upstairs. He realized that he must revert to the national frugality of his homeland if he was to recover his good health and spirits; and this he did, making a painstaking study of his needs in the way of food. The result had been a vegetarian diet for the most part, though he might from time to time have a glass of wine as a politeness; he cut down starch to the minimum, and cut out meat, though not fish. But this was strictly a health plan, and had nothing to do with any special religious bias; or only in the sense that the Taoist notion of immortality was implicated as a long-term consideration. Of this I was eager to learn more, and was delighted to find someone who had read these philosophers in the original and could orient my thinking in their regard.

7

This of course had a direct bearing on the genesis and structure of his book, which lay there waiting for us, spread out upon my work-table. But while we ate he gave me, so to speak, a background sketch of the recent history of the ideas it embodied.[1] He began with the invasion and conquest of China by the Manchurians. These fine gentlemen with their Spartan philistinism had ruled for a matter of eighty-eight years, and during their tenure had most successfully succeeded in muffling, indeed practically eradicating, all outward manifestation of Taoism and burned all Taoist books except the *Tao Te Ching*, possibly because it was too profound for the barbarians to recognize its significance. Luckily also for the Taoists they did not have the propensity for certain set factors – temples, rituals, uniforms, etc. There was nothing to pinpoint them for persecution. 'The true Taoists . . . there was no distinguishing feature about them except, if you like, a certain look in the eye – a Taoist look! A look in the eye of the mind, so to speak! You could hardly persecute a mere Look!' So saying, Chang gave me a Taoist look as a sample, and I saw at once what he meant. It was a great little look, full of mischievous impudence, of irony and laughter. It was a look of sardonic complicity – it shared an amused and slanting consciousness of how precious the Unspoken was. It was like the first link between human beings acknowledging their partnership in the whole of process. *Diable!* It was the damnedest look I have ever shared with a human being – leaving aside two women who seemed to be naturally endowed the whole time with such a look by the gods. I realized that I was looking into the eyes of Chuang Tzu, my favourite philosopher – the Groucho Marx of Taoist philosophy. It was the eye of the Great Paradox, so to speak. There is nothing to be said about this sort of thing – it is Taoism, and the minute you try to say something explicit about it you damage it, like clumsily trying to pick up a rare butterfly in your fingers. Here you are in the region of the Indian *non-this-non-that business*. What we made and shared as we talked thus was a magnificent meal – the amused, penetrating, conspiratorial Look seemed to have got into the very food and by now we had already begun to chaff each other, which is the best mark of friendship.

Taoism is such a privileged brand of eastern philosophy that one would be right to regard it as an aesthetic view of the universe rather than a purely institutional one. A Taoist was the joker in the pack, the poet on the hearth. His angle of inclination depended upon a simple proposition, namely that the world was a Paradise, and one was under an obligation to realize it as fully as possible before being forced to quit it. The big imperative in the matter was that there should be no waste, not a drop, in the course of this great feast of innocent breath. In an obscure sort of way the concept of immortal human *bonheur* had crept into the Taoist mind. They chose to leave the grand question of supreme bliss, of perfect beatitude, to the higher grades of the religious hierachy, and stick to the world as IS – or that is what they seemed to say. But how was this desirable state of immortality in this life to be brought about? One could not just guzzle the world away, for mental indigestion would soon supervene. The greatest delicacy of judgement, the greatest refinement of intention was to replace the brutish automatism with which most of us continue to exist, stuck like prehistoric animals in the sludge of our non-awareness.

The realization comes at the point where the Taoist experiences inside himself a new state of pure heed – the notion that the whole of eternity could be compromised by a careless word, by a mere inattention, by the untimely trembling of a leaf! We speak of people who have realized themselves because we know that Real things only happen to Real People, though it seems very unlucky. As for the perfect rapture – it was towards the poem (the ideogram of a perfected apprehension) that Taoism of this kind tended. That was why Chang was slightly irritated by the heavy conceptual lumber, the wearisome prolixity of Indian thought with its eternal accretion of detail, its overwhelming density. Such an apparatus often bred scholars not sages, pedants not poets. What the Chinese mind had brought to this over-elaborated marvel was precisely the resilient humour which it lacked. The difference lay not in the end but in the means. I could see that the Taoism of Chang was born of the smile of Kasyapa – that none too diligent student whom Buddha sent to the top of the form because, while he, the Master, was still in full discourse, he happened to catch the eye of this young man, and to surprise upon his face the Taoist smile! There was no need to go on talking for it was clear from this one smiling glance that Kasyapa had twigged the whole matter. Buddha handed him the flower he was holding in his hand and told him to get the hell out of the class. So Kasyapa, who found the Indians such fearful bores and so lacking in humour, set out for China with only the Taoist smile for baggage. And out of this exchange of looks grew the Far Eastern variety of the Buddhist reality – and later the remarkable short cut of the Zen jump which completely bypassed the jungle of Indian metaphysics while encapsulating the real essence of the teaching. Somewhere in the heart of the matter was a principle of right apprehension which was there for the discovering; after that one could breathe in the whole universe with every breath. Treat the earth as perfume? Well, a scent does not try to get itself appreciated by an act of will, even though it 'knows' in its essence that it was born for just that. Congruence, appropriateness, it was our job to capture the whole thing when it was bliss side up, so to speak. I read all this into Chang's text. To become at long last accredited to the whole of nature!

But these and other matters got themselves quite entangled in the question of cookery – for Chang had now begun to feel his feet in the pleasant kitchen with its red-tiled floor. To me he delegated the task of cutter-up for the carefully washed vegetables; in defence too of my gallant Indians, among whom I spent the first ten years of my existence, I introduced a few touches of India to the sauce – curry and ginger – which met with approval. We had found nuts and raisins in the market as well, while my guest was eager to explore a few of the cheeses of France. It was a pleasant and fruitful work, assembling all these deliciously steamed still crunchy vegetables. It was also a symbolic meeting place of the two great cuisines of the world – French and Chinese.

II

Among so many subjects we were apt to lose our way from time to time —
Chang replying to my eager questions no less eagerly; he seemed glad to
have someone at hand with whom he could discuss these matters, albeit in
English. My knowledge though highly provisional and sketchy was quite a
help towards my understanding of his text, which was an outline of a sort
of love-therapy — not rigidly schematic and fossilized like the Kama Sutra,
though much upon the same lines. I asked him about yoga and told him I
dabbled in the Indian method. 'I do Chinese yoga,' he said. 'It's a bit different — more fluent, less static.' Waving a wooden spoon he did a couple of
swooping figures, not unlike ballroom dancing, gliding out into the old
glassed-in verandah like an ice-skater. I tried to copy him to see how it felt.
At that moment the morose existentialist gardener who sometimes works
for me came down the drive, and peering in saw me apparently waltzing
with a Chinaman. We did not see him ourselves. But his nerve was badly
shaken by the sight and he retreated to the village tavern. Oblivious to all
this we danced on, Chang and I, until a simmering noise called us back to
the cooking pots.

III

The question of immortality also raised its head early on in the conversations and I found that my guest was absolutely convinced that it was not a figure of speech, that it was on the menu, so to speak, though factually it could only be achieved by the greatest sages. There existed records, however, which pointed that way. As far as he was concerned all he wished to illuminate in the text under consideration was the fact that if a man adapted himself to the Taoist view seriously – he could easily top the hundred, and might expect without being specially gifted to live to 150. In such a life there was no reason why he should not expect to make love happily well into his nineties, as well as keep all or most of his teeth. Everything was connected to his diet, both spiritual and physical. 'I myself propose to live to 120 years at least. If I had started this technique much earlier I could expect to go the full way. But the question of food and of sexual love is paramount, and here the book has something to teach us. You will understand that I have assembled and translated these texts first for my own pleasure and then as a work of advocacy for a world which quietly accepts to be flung on the scrap-heap around the age of fifty; which loses its sexual abilities soon after forty in many cases; and which uses the orgasm as a sort of yardstick of well-being, when it can, after forty, be restrained and re-educated in the service of insight rather than trivialized in mere pleasure ... '

This, then, was a sort of treatise on *coitus reservatus* and the transmutation of physical love into a delight based in physical contact, cherishing rather than ravishing. I could see too that he believed that we in the West used the orgasm rather as a weapon; it proved to the individual's ego that he was dominating his partner. Sex could be used assertively. In these ancient texts it was emphasized over and over again that the man's sperm (the same Chinese character stands for sperm and for essence, just to confuse the western wits) was extremely precious; it should be treated as such and conserved as much as possible after the age of forty if one was going to take the long haul towards immortality. Chang himself had adopted the ancient technique. He limited himself to one orgasm per one hundred love-encounters, approximately, and he managed to make love to several girls in the same day! It sounded absolutely outlandish to my western mind; yet here in the text was the advice and guidance of the ancient Love-Masters who counselled this method of preserving health and longevity. The organization of the woman is so different that she is fortified rather than depleted by the orgasm and consequently she did not play so great a part in the book, except as a fully responsive and cherishing partner for the man. But it was clear that she would profit handsomely from this system! Chang felt that with the important changes in the sexual scene based on the invention of the Pill in the West, the time was ripe for a work of Chinese scholarship along these traditional lines. But how to get over his meaning without giving the impression of lubricity or indelicacy? For the Chinese mind sexuality was the rarest flower of the spiritual *gai savoir* – and compared to the odious prurience and brutality of the western attitude it is difficult to situate it clearly for what it is – the meeting ground of two perfections. That is why, for example, there was nothing in the text about oblong considerations like homosexuality, lesbianism, deviations so dear to the contemporary mind. In the context of the Tao (for the purposes of his text) they did not really exist. Or if they did, they did not concern his theme – for the love-partners described in the text enjoyed the functional polarity of male and female with the Tao. The sexual act was a love act which meshed them into the whole of cosmic process; not a pillow-fight between egos determined to dominate each other. The whole sexual gymkhana of the West – the eternal plucking at the ego – filled Chang with sadness, and I could very well see why.

The image he used, the simple analogy which in a way echoed the double snakes twined round the shaft of the spine (caduceus-wise), was the ordinary light bulb with its twining filaments which between them rise to the base of the skull and confer light. Why write a treatise to include everything that was out of phase – all the gynandromorph forms which produced only darkness wherever nature had slipped? The treatise was upon love achieved, not love among the ruins of our sexual culture. I am afraid that his analysis of our sad state seemed perfectly accurate when he laid the blame at the door of Christianity – with its cult of the ego, of original sin, of the wrathful God, and so on. How pure and kindly the simple Chinese ordinances seemed when one thought of our plight in the West. It was most instructive to me to see ourselves through his Chinese eyes. The aesthete in Chang was disgusted and terrified when he thought of the sexual atmosphere of cruelty and ugliness which he found in the arts; but he was just as shocked when he thought of the bulging dustbins of Los Angeles and London, the reckless improvidence which led us to pollute and devastate our natural inheritance upon earth in a perverse almost deliberate search for unhappiness. The question of sexual deviation led him on his side to question me about such matters. Was there much homosexuality in Tibet? No, but plenty in Mount Athos and the Vatican! Could it be that the element of narcissism which is at the base of it in the Freudian analysis is vastly strengthened by the Christian code, the cult of the Luciferian will to power? He laughed, and admitted that it could be true.

'People want to have done with sex because it has brought them nothing but shame and disappointment; and its misuse has brought them to a premature old age. They lack desire themselves and because of the fearful things they eat they smell so awful that nobody feels like caressing them. Old age is a dreadful thing in the West. No wonder it is feared, no wonder the old are put away in remote flats or old-age communities and left to die. They have no further function, and they have forfeited the joy which should be theirs.' (I thought to myself: Why has the Dalai Lama got no Oedipus Complex? Answer: Because he has no mother and no father. The buck stops there!) But meanwhile what of the lovers – the Taoist lovers caught up in their eternal embrace, gathered into the spiral momentum of the All, the cosmic rhythm as it ripples slowly along its trajectory of yang and yin, back and forth, the pendulum of mother nature? What about Jack loves Jill? Chang grew irritated. 'The lovers in the book are simply the representatives of a natural process. Of course Jack can love Jill and write love poems to her, not to mention to recite acrostics with rather questionable meanings, in order to make her laugh. But that aspect of things concerns their personalities, it is in the domain of the novel. This treatise presumes them to be The Perfect Couple, perfectly slotted into the science of the love-yoga: The Tao. It is beyond the man-eat-dog stage in human affairs. My lovers are the Nonpareil, the Peerless Lovers of the Taoist scheme. We shouldn't address silly questions to people about them. Theirs is a condition to be aspired to, even if we never reach it.' Simple as the sap travelling through the veins of a tree. Sadism, masochism, why be bothered with them except to regret that with them nature went out of true, and it was our fault? You become what you believe. The Taoist lovers, then, were ego-less; they were human embodiments of cosmic process; one was silly even to want to call them Jack and Jill when in reality they were sleepwalking yangs and yins ... At this moment there was a power-cut and I thought of Chang's pleasure and wonder every time he switched on the electric light with its 'filaments of gratified if disembodied desire'. The gratification of the lovers lay on a different plane; by dint of mastering the orgasm one raised love to a higher frequency. One prolonged life, the immortal life which one was in honour bound to try and realize upon earth ... How difficult it was to express all this in a way which might make good sense to someone brought up in the West, by the canons of a culture whose language was based on dichotomy. But perhaps more important even than this was that the ancient Taoist view of sexuality suggested that they considered it to be the basic mechanism upon which the happy and healthy functioning of the whole man depended. Hence the role of the Love-Masters whose field of investigation was the whole psycho-physical situation. 'It is after all not so far from the psycho-somatic approach of modern medicine – only that contains no built-in cosmic doctrine designed to pull out the thorns of the ego.'

Talking, arguing and eating thus in little bits we tackled the text piece-meal – there was so much to explain to me about the language of the original and the attitude of its ancient therapists. Behind the whole science lay a theory of fulcrum and realization which made the Buddhist adventure – even the Indian – one of the most extraordinary intellectual forays into the unknown. In a world of living things devoted to preying upon one another – and full of the savage defence mechanisms engendered by fear – the Buddhist proposed to make himself ever more defenceless against fate, thus unlocking the karmic spring, 'the will power of desirelessness' in E. Graham Howe's phrase, which in fact modified his field of action by submission. To move thus towards the moon of his non-being, rolling with the punch, so to speak, he found an inner mechanism which ensured that he came back into his fair course at last by the law of the opposites. But all this to us was apparently going against the laws of evolution and causality as they seemed to be consti-tuted in the theories of the survival of the fittest. Was the law of the jungle not what we had been led to believe? It was as if the yogi wished to re-establish an anterior state of mind, a plant-like acquiescence which perhaps had dominated early man – before the Aristotelian gift of con-sciousness bugged him, bogged him down with its cogito-ergo-impulse-inhibition-machine. I wondered if this was what Old Empedocles of Sicily had meant by saying that the first men were trees – perhaps he meant plants? After all, man came out of water originally. The jewel of intuition realized from the lotus anchored in the mud of primal consciousness?

Snap! the lights came on again and simultaneously Chang brought his great heap of whistling vegetables to table and we fell to, while he told me how strange he had found the New World at first, how difficult the language – not grammatically but conceptually. And how funny! Ah! the blessed irony of the Chinese mind! I realized then that it was quite different from that of the bandy-legged and banausic Japs on one side, and the twanging tingling Indian sophists on the other. The man who can see the world with wondering irony tends to be a good conductor, someone on whom one can count! 'Tell me about Christianity,' he said, with his mouth full. 'Well, to begin with the Last Supper – it was not a vegetarian meal, you will have noticed.' I uncorked a wholesome bottle of St Saturnin and loaded my glass. Chang shook his head and said, 'You are drinking a little too much. We must try something on you.' I did not know what he meant, and I hoped it would be Chinese hypnotism which would influence my subliminal self to start cutting down. But all these ideas had excited me immeasurably and I needed the wine to carry out the architectural design of this simple but delicious meal, combining China, France and India in almost equal parts. 'Tell me about your education,' I said, and he laughed. He had heard the voice of the schools in full bombination. He had heard dons in California 'explicating' Shakespeare; he had seen chain-smoking American yogis reverently watching television in the Lotus pose . . . He was funny about it and quite unmalicious. And now from his little air-bag he produced, somewhat to my surprise, a formidable collection of tubes of various vitamins with which he proceeded to dose himself. 'Well, who would have thought it?' I said in a shocked tone, and he grinned. He said, 'There are many good things here in the West, and I see no reason why I should not use them. Your science has done some excellent work on diets, the role of cholesterol, the carbohydrates and so on. I do not propose to be bigoted. They are indeed a great help if you want to stay as slim as I am – short cuts, if you like, but useful.'

He had already spent some years in the field against the Japanese when his family decided to send him to the Americas; he was a bold and very industrious boy, and soon learned English and became a Canadian citizen. He also made his disastrous excursions into the dietary system of the Anglo-Saxons with the results already recorded. He had obviously retarded his immortality a bit by this lapse! But in part it all served a purpose, for while he was engaged in trying to cure himself he started to look up old Chinese texts which he found in the libraries of the New World and of England, which he frequently visited. He discovered that there was more to Taoism than just a religion or philosophy; there was a medical rationale as well, and an index to the frugal joys of whole living on earth. The texts had all been widely dispersed and he had had a task assembling them into what he hoped might be a coherent whole – a theory of health within the concept of the universal Tao. This, then, became the subject-matter of our long and scattered conversations. The few days he spent with me seemed endless, they passed in beguiling slow motion – time in full extension, so to speak. When I say 'long discussions' I mean really long: we knocked off only to light a fire and cook a meal – we ate about five times a day. I suppose we slept for a few hours – he found the guest room cold and asked if he might make a hot-water bottle. This was a sign of degeneracy I told him – surely his yoga kept him warm? It did, but unfortunately he had had a tiny sip of wine, and alcohol was fatal for the balance of the organism. He disdained however my offer of a massive rubber water bottle in favour of his own tiny one. I found that he carried a small supply of milk in one of those containers that campers use to ice their meals – thermic sacks I think they are called. He drank away his milk with reverence before filling the container with boiling water. I had the impression that night and day had become one – after a short sleep one might get up to discuss the text once more. Once we absently went for a walk. (As for the tiny hot-water bottle, it hardly covered the soles of his feet.) But discuss the text as we might, he was always shooting down my rhapsodic fancies and pulling me down to earth with a typically Chinese sense of priorities. 'To hell with nirvana and fulcrums and all that,' he would say. 'That is all self-evident, but what we must not lose sight of is that the book deals with exploiting this life on earth to the absolute full, so that we leave nothing behind, not even a sigh. The ordinary life-span is too short to fully enjoy this world; we could and should expand it immeasurably to give ourselves time. It is down to earth all this, and extremely practical.'

He had had the luck during the course of these studies to win the acquaintance of Joseph Needham, our greatest Sinologue, whose multi-volumed study of Chinese science is almost complete and is certainly one of the great books of our time.[2] Needham had promised him a preface and a postscript to his own book if he would assemble it in scholarly fashion and clear terms. This of course was a great compliment and he appreciated its full extent. But of course the trouble was that one part of this theme was highly abstract, and the other almost elementary. The basic problem on the practical side was the culture of the orgasm – a culture characterized by premature emission on the part of the male and a corresponding frustration on the part of the female. This could and should be righted, and the ancient texts of the Love-Masters gave precise hints and rules, while diet and religious observance framed and illustrated the whole matter of love-making as part of a cosmic science. From the so-called Cartesian point of view (so much valued by the French) all this seemed highly aberrant; but I found that it made good sense to me. I was able to verify from my own personal experience the fact that there was, as Chang says, a great difference between an ejaculation and an orgasm. In the love-making of which the Taoist doctrine spoke there could supervene an orgasm without loss of the vital Taoist essence. It was a question not only of conscious practice but of rapport, of attachment – the whole precious transaction was lifted to a new height of intensity which could endure for hours at a time, if necessary, because the two spirits remained enmeshed in each other. I had twice realized this experience – which presupposes an attachment so intense, so profound that if it did not meet with its response, its opposite, the resulting spring-back, the disappointment, would imperil reason itself!

It came, it seemed to me, as the result of the right kind of piety in love – piety which had nothing to do with a conventional religiosity. I had known it with one person – she had carried the tantric look with her, right into the midst of her death, like a standard. For a whole night the blue eyes continued to regard me with their impish felicity – the sapphire-blue regard with its privileged smile. In the whole of this fine transaction, I realized then there had been no place for self-gratification of a selfish kind. I was face to face with the blue flower of a perfected knowledge. Only towards dawn the look became first sea-green, and then softly vitreous, it began to lose its pollen, to cloud over. I woke from those hours of riveted attention feeling profoundly informed by that serene tantric regard from the other side of death. To have been loved – I suddenly realized what a great compliment it was! Yet amusingly enough so often we had not been aware whether we had actually *made* love or not – so rapt had been the insight, so dense the communion of presence and touch. Yes, I knew what Chang's text was getting at, though I wondered whether such notions would make any headway in an age such as ours, where such a spiritual state was as rare as the physical one was – orgasm without ejaculation! How could one put this over to monotheistic Christians who had been twisted by sanctimoniousness into the arthritic form of crucifixes? It had died with the last cathar, that look!

The quiddity of the Tao is in its quizzical stance. (The little god is called *Coitus Absconditus*!) My friend sat so perfectly still, watching me as I paced up and down, that I thought he had perhaps fallen asleep. 'You are very hard on Christianity,' he said at last, and I knew he was right. But it was all due to a mental jolt I received in my seventh or eighth year in Darjiling, where for a couple of years I had been placed in a Jesuit public school. It was a very good school and the good fathers were fine men – there was no propaganda. They preached by example only, and the example they gave was a high one. No, it was not they who gave me the shock. We Protestants numbered about forty children, and we were supposed to worship in town at the Church of England chapel. But one day while passing the Jesuit school chapel I found the door ajar and tiptoed inside, curious as children are. In the deep gloom I came upon a life-size figure of Christ crucified hanging over the altar, liberally blotched with blood and perfectly pig-sticked and thorn-hatted. An indescribable feeling of horror and fear welled up in me. So *this* was what those austerely garbed and bearded priests worshipped in this dense gloom among the flowers and candles! It was hardly a logical sequence of feelings and senti-ments – it was quite spontaneous and unformulated. But the horror remained with me always; and later on, when my father decreed that I must go to England for my education, I felt that he was delivering me into the hands of these sadists and cannibals, men who could worship this brutal and savage effigy on the Christian cross. Naturally I could not put all this into words for many a year, but at that precise moment I knew that henceforward I would never bring myself to trust anyone who called himself a Christian and so invoke this doom-laden symbol of unhappi-ness! How right I was! So far nothing has ever come my way which might persuade me to modify this somewhat decisive though perhaps absurd view.[3] The main road which passed the school in Darjiling ran along the side of the playing-fields; the sight of Tibetan lamas setting off on their long pilgrimages to the distant plains of India was a familiar one. Smiling, as if sauntering through the pages of *Kim*, they whirled their small prayer-wheels. I have had them on my mind ever since and can still hear the noise of the little brass wheels as they whirred out their prayers. But I had to make a wide detour to rediscover them, the lamas! A lion, I was thrown to the Christians!

*   *   *

So, page by page, the text opened itself to our study, while the arguments and explanations spread out sideways from it, like crabs. Chang was delighted to hear that even old Rabelais had devoted thought to the matter of longevity, wondering if one could not 'try how long an ingenious and agreeable man might last, if taken good care of'. Presumably the same sort of formula would apply – breathing, diet, husbanding of sexuality. Chang's Taoist answers must have seemed on the face of it somewhat extravagant; yet here in the book were texts and pronouncements by the old masters of this love-craft which suggested quite the contrary. I was cutting up leeks as these ideas came under scrutiny and inadvertently threw out large sections of the outer leaves as I prepared them. Horrified, Chang gave a sort of little chirp – a Chinese sob – and dived down to the dustbin to recover them crying angrily: 'You are wasting again; and you *know* how firm my Taoist principles are!' There was heartbreak in his voice and I felt chastened and sorry. He took the discarded leaves and smoothed them delicately out with his fingers – as if they might have had a precious message graven on them. He washed them. 'They are too coarse and old, Jolan,' I remonstrated, but he shook his head and pursed his lips. He rolled them as one would a big tobacco leaf and taking the sharpest of the knives he cut them as finely as possible. He repeated for the hundredth time, 'Anything is eatable if cut up small enough!' I was proud of one thing however: to have reconverted him to ginger – it was a long time since he had used any in his cooking; also curry, I had some fresh curry from Madras – fresh from the armpits of Khrishna, so to speak. He was less charitable to the wines in the house, and would not touch coffee. But he watched me indulgently as I drank, and toasting him I said, 'I am suffering from a case of repressed longevity.' But he only smiled and shook his head sadly, saying: 'You are drinking too much; it makes you reason falsely and disturbs your yoga balance – not to mention making you fat . . . ' He was right, of course, but then the Good God gave us reason to make fools of ourselves with, and I did not want to be left behind. In a certain subterranean way this talk of the Tao – of the prelapsarian *déclic* which would enable one to turn the key of immortality in the lock – chimed in my mind with some old ideas I had had once about the nature of the poetic act. I felt that it was as if one were making the orgasm more and more conscious with each poem, exhausting, so to speak, the simple amnesia provoked by the ejaculation *per se*. Perhaps, without knowing it, I had been very close to the heart of the Tao of sex, as preached by my friend here, who was now sitting at the kitchen table looking at me in rather a curious way. He wore a look of devoted concentration on his face. Then I saw with surprise that there was a glass of wine before him. 'I am going to drink with you,' he said, 'just to see what you see in it, if anything.' Knowing his principles, and the highly strung and delicate state of health he enjoyed from the exercise of such radical precautions against gluttony, I did not believe him at first. I drank off a swig. He at once followed suit. I drank another. So did he. He made an awful face as he did so, but he seemed quite determined to commit suicide in this nauseating way – was it to register a reproach or a warning? I said nothing but went on talking of the pre-Adamic structure of the psyche and other matters, of the same sort, drinking all the while. He was imitating me. When I replenished my glass he held his out for a refill. 'Come off it,' I said, 'I know it's bad for you. Are you just trying to shame me?' He shook his head and answered, 'No, I am just trying something on you.' I took a swig; he took a swig. In this way we finished dinner together drinking glass for glass. Of course it was an unequal struggle for I was in training while he, poor Taoist... He began to get unsteady and giggly; he found my jokes inordinately funny. I began to wonder if I should have to carry him up to bed. I felt that it was about time that the West made some cultural contribution to the Taoist scene, so I gave the Great Vampire Chortle – the sound with which I greet every unforeseen adversity in life. 'What an extraordinary sound,' he said. 'What does it do?' I answered. 'It clears the air and clears the head; I have adapted it from Greek and Tibetan sources. Those who learn the Great Chortle are saved. Try it.' He poised himself as if about to jump over a precipice and produced a very tolerable imitation of my chortle. Together we practised it a bit while we drank, until the plaster began to come off the ceiling. It was lucky that the morose existentialist gardener did not choose that moment to peer in from the balcony...

Altogether it was a splendid evening, full of variety, and yet full of this directed concentration with which my friend sought to imprint my psyche. I could feel the fall-out getting into the wine – but not fast enough to prevent my drinking the statutory amount for a great evening. Afterwards he explained to me the dynamic of this little act – which is called just 'sitting' in Chinese. It is part of a health-giving mechanism which is within the powers of anyone and everyone. The aim is to modify conduct in a fruitful sense – if you have a friend who is harming himself by a certain line of conduct. By sitting close to him and concentrating on that conduct you can, so to speak, meditate him into another groove, another shift. Like switching points on a railway. It has nothing to do with professional medical healing where the doctor imposes his will and his

21

treatment on the sick man; nor is it the imposition of one's own will-power upon the patient. As he explained it, in the sitting technique one simply mentally steps into the character of your friend as one steps into a boat and starts trying to steer it. Obviously wind and current play their part. But by an act of friendly passivity one sometimes can prod them to modify fruitless conduct and reorient themselves ... I labour this point because for a whole month and a half after the departure of Jolan my intake of red wine dropped back equably, without stress, to four or five glasses a day – against a customary four or five pints. But the influence wore off after a while. Yet it was like post-hypnotic suggestion, and I have since tried it myself on someone – just sitting, meditating, not saying any-thing – with distinct results in the right direction. I must say though that the wine gave a rosy glow to the text and its ideas of harmony and bounty; it made men and women natural allies, sexual partners in a cosmic technique. Indeed I saw that some of the great Love-Masters to the Emperors were in fact women whose advice was sought. Great Love-Consultants, their names have come down through these texts full of the fragrance and ardour of a language which has never known prudishness or prurience in matters of love. We spoke of the breathing and yoga side of the matter (it was in this field that the wine was robbing me of control). But I had grasped the central notion as far as I could judge, in the Chinese context. I asked myself what differentiates the conduct of the acrobat from that of the yogi. The acrobat can perform feats of physical skill superior to the yogi's postures however complicated, yet it leads him nowhere because the issue of his skill is not one of virtue involving a cosmic principle. He is unaware of the poetic lodestar the yogi captures – the magnetic field which he enters.

Jolan Chang gave a chortle. It was sad, but also in a strange way con-soling, to find that during a whole historic period in China itself the notation of the Tao had been lost, the link between men and women had been broken. They had become vampires, the women; and the men lost and effeminate; the whole cultural and political scheme of things had lost its equilibrium. The states foundered in anarchy and dissolution. The germ in the wheat had gone bad. A dark age settled over the whole land. According to my friend Chinese history could offer more than one example of this sort of collapse of the historic consciousness together with the corresponding recovery which followed with the swing of the pendulum, for nothing lasts for ever. Would we live to see our own age recover its wits? I wondered. Everything in nature hangs by a hair ...
'Embark on the Tao and you won't have a moment's peace, because it

demands unremitting application and comprehension and balance.' (That is what Lao Tsu was saying.) You are like a tightrope-walker high above a city; yet with practice you can one day do the walk blindfold, without vertigo. Against reason I have always believed so. It was encouraging that Chang also supported this interpretation of the poem.

Before we turned in that evening for the usual shortened sleep I witnessed an amusing outbreak of Chinese humour, which came over my friend in a wave at the sight of an ashtray. By some singular coincidence the gypsies and traders had been bringing all sorts of esoteric trinkets into the village for the Saturday market. Esoteric in the sense that there were flower vases of glass marked 'Birmingham', marvellously life-like Indian roses made of silk, and so on. Among all this stuff I had happened upon a couple of little bamboo ashtrays, pleasant of shape and with a colour-wash design on them depicting a bush, a river, the figure of a girl holding a fishing rod. The style was very debased but the idiom was quite inescapably Chinese. In a search for matches by the kitchen sink Chang hit upon one of these trinkets. He uttered an exclamation of curiosity and picked it up to examine it. He turned it over. On the back it had a legend in English which read 'Made in Taiwan'. Something came over him as he read the words and he turned to me, helpless with laughter, pointing at the phrase with his finger, speechless with mirth. In a sort of way I could follow the contours of this cosmic joke – if one thought of the immensity and complexity and age of China and the triviality of contemporary power politics in the hands of American cowboys, or evangelical tycoons with Las Vegas souls . . . Yes, it merited the laughter. It was so infectious, his laugh, that I was forced to join in, and together we doubled up. laughing until our sides ached and I implored him to stop.

'Taiwan,' he gasped helplessly.

'Taiwan,' I echoed, just as helpless. There was no need for a further gloze on the matter, though what the gardener would have made of our behaviour I have no idea. For some time afterwards whenever Jolan caught sight of this little saucer with its debased and disinherited scribble he gave an involuntary chuckle.

He had brought a certain amount of ancillary documentation with him of the Kinseyfied kind, and while I have nothing against the statistical approach I know how untrustworthy it can be when used as a basis for analysis, and also how few questionnaires are ever really truthfully filled in. Chang did not agree about this. He had seen some good results in the quantitative field. Yes, but were we harking back to a lost innocence or forward to a shift of principle in the West which might modify, not merely conduct, the inward dispositions of the psyche – given the new permissive (so-called) changes of sexual behaviour? Chang said, 'Look, I am not selling anything. I offer you here a sheaf of texts which adds up to a fairly coherent system devoted to health and psychic balance.'

We spoke, I remember, a good deal about Henry Miller and his ailments which interested Chang very much, for he admired his work and had grasped the central implication in it which so many people still miss. Miller himself has said it somewhere in an interview: 'My books are not about sex, they are about self-liberation.' Chang was delighted to hear that he was in his eighties and convinced that with a little care he might top the hundred – after which, apparently, things got very much easier. He said he would like to give him some free advice strictly as a gerontologist, and to this end I dug out a typewriter and started to take dictation – which resulted in a long and detailed letter about how to conserve his energies and faculties. There were some Chinese herbs he mentioned like the Gin Seng root – but Miller was already taking these. The marvellous thing was the old writer's joyful optimism in spite of a wonky leg with a plastic artery which didn't really do the work of the real one which they had removed; and then one eye was also giving him trouble. Chang assured me that all this was quite remediable if his advice were followed, so we packed off a long letter to Miller with all speed.

After this we started cooking again and my companion said, 'After we have eaten I shall give you a very special pleasure. I had the luck to pick up a piece of Sung ceramic in an antiquary's shop in London for a few pence – he had not recognized it.' Duly, when we had finished our meal, he hunted through his little air-satchels, taking, in passing, a fanatical sip of milk from his bottle, and then produced a small dark-brown vase; there was nothing on it in the way of engraving or decoration, and indeed, there seemed to be little enough *to* it – one has seen lathe-turned objects of precision which have a certain snug efficiency of shape without being aesthetically haunting. I said so, but he only smiled. 'But you are not looking. Just look at it, like a shape, like a shadow or a cloud.' He picked it up on three fingers and with a turn of the wrist presented it towards the window with its sunlight. 'How do you know it is a Sung piece?' He smiled again. 'The proportions – there is no other distinguishing mark. That is why the antiquary missed it. He is like a blind man who has to proceed from the familiar touch of things. Here, if one only had touch one could not tell what it was. Try looking *into* it and feel the proportions, feel the way it was potted like a bird's egg.' After a while I began to see in a dim way what he saw; it was rather like a theorem in geometry. Then I

space, only a conditional space, as well as a certain longing for the security and certainty of the cage from which it has escaped. But most of these excursions into the outer reaches of philosophy were of no use to the present manuscript which he preferred to keep quite simple, as a monograph, without any didactic or ethical overtones. As for the Tao and the whole complex of Chinese thought: it was I who was to benefit by leading him far afield in the moments when we broke off to eat, sleep, discuss, walk. It was enriching for me to discuss these old life-shaping passions like Lao Tsu and Chuang Tzu with someone who had fully grasped the original.

In a general sense too I had repaid my debt to him precisely because in talking round and round the whole subject as we had done I had illuminated for him many areas of our Occidental thought which needed his consideration if he was to make his subject matter clear and penetrating to his western reader. I had tested the text, in some aspects somewhat sketchy, against every kind of objection, and he was glad that I had not found it wanting. Time, too, was running out and he was expected at Cambridge, where he would be put up by a friend under rather Spartan conditions, which sometimes resulted in his having to sleep on the floor! But he looked after his clothes and his general *tenue* as punctiliously as a cat. Despite all the offers of the maid to wash his clothes or iron them he preferred to tend them himself, passing a wet cloth over them, or a warm iron. When I thought of the simple way he travelled, sleeping sitting up in trains, and so on, I was struck by how spruce he managed to keep himself. I of course regretted his going so soon. His book had formed a sort of bond between me and my own youthful preoccupations which had all got themselves crystallized round the notion of Tao. It led me back like a plumbline to that remote and far off day by the blue Ionian Sea when I said to myself with astonishment, 'Why goodness me, I must be a *Taoist*!' It explained also the nagging sense of disjunction I had always felt in the West, the sense of being a savage; and also the guilt of feeling that I was playing a part and was unequal to my responsibilities as a Christian believer, and I longed to conform since I loved my mother and father. Yet the awakening, *pour ainsi dire*, was not just of a poetic order – though if I call it 'religious' I mean it rather in the anthropological sense and not in the denominational. After I awoke into poetry I had the feeling that from thenceforward I could do nothing that was wholly frivolous, everything made sense; even if I were to commit evil it would still be purposeful . . . Then there came another thought which was equally gratuitous, arriving from nowhere. 'The poet is one whom death cannot surprise, for he has taken up an imaginative emplacement within it by his poems.' A kid, I had fallen into milk with a vengeance!

'Have you any food you don't want?' The question brought me back to myself. 'Because I could take it with me. I eat very lightly when I am travelling.' Together we examined the fridge. He took a lascivious sip of milk to see if it had turned or not. No! Could he take it with him? He reverently poured it into his little hot-water bottle. There were a couple of apples, a small fragment of cheese and a couple of biscuits and a tomato. I calculated that it would just about have kept a mouse alive for a night or so. 'This will last me three days at least,' said Chang running his eye over the assembled items. I pictured him in the wastes of Cambridge nibbling at this fare and blowing on his fingers for warmth; but like all good yoga men he hardly felt the cold. 'I shall be all right.' I had intended to take him to a station myself but at the last moment I had a notification for a long-distance telephone call which I could not countermand. So I called the village taxi which came scratching and scrawling into the drive on all the loose gravel. 'Well,' he said, giving me the benefit of a final Taoist look accompanied by a smile of friendly complicity. 'Thank you for the whole trip. It's been a memorable meeting, no?' Indeed it had, and I felt so despondent at the sight of him leaving that I quite forgot to give him a farewell Chortle. He strung his belongings around him and donned his light overcoat and the ski bonnet of soft wool. 'We'll meet again in London,' he said, and I agreed. Then the taxi bore him off into the night while I stood in the garden for a while, thinking of his book and listening to the whistle of the owls as they came whirring down in search of field-mice or bats.

So ended my first Taoist visitation, and as the spring wore on to summer I began to be increasingly taken up with other problems of the ordinary kind. But from time to time I received a call from Jolan Chang to report progress on the book. He had found some delightful and appropriate illustrations, the preface and postface were excellent, and so on. I contributed a note for the sleeve, but I promised more substantial help later on which, by a series of trifling mishaps, I was unable to supply at the right time. But the book appeared and did well, receiving a serious if slightly reserved English press. In France, however, its critics were more enthusiastic and its public, for the most part young, very enthusiastic. Apparently it made sense, even to people habitually subjected to the fraudulent cat's cradle of the dialectic or to the hiccups of Tel Quel! But it was too simple and unpretentious a book to get up powerful tensions of an intellectual kind. In fact, one would have to have an inkling of the value of breath to be struck by it, I suppose; or to have taken soundings already and come to some conclusions about the meaning of silence . . . But at all events the little bookshop which abuts the old Sorbonne told me that it was much in demand. Chang went back to his great flat and his collection – not to mention his tiny gnome of a daughter – and our correspondence lapsed; I had several journeys ahead of me. But I was sorry to have failed him at the London end. Happily the support of Joseph Needham had given the book the prestige it needed for its launching.

IV

The desultory autumn set in – the economy of France had begun to founder with the resulting labour troubles due to the high cost of petrol. The Arabs had overturned the apple cart of our economy and there would be no way back to prosperity and full employment in my lifetime. Well, what did it matter after sixty? In Paris, sauntering the *quais*, I came upon a Collected Oscar Wilde and to my astonishment saw in it a review of the *Tao Te Ching* by his hand; paradoxically enough it had been written for a ladies' fashion magazine of which he had once been editor. It was, if my memory serves me right, a review of the first London translation, by Giles. And Wilde's sympathetic little notice suggested that he had thoroughly understood the doctrines of the old sage. It must have dated from his more impecunious period when he was forced to turn to journalism to make ends meet. (He wasn't the only one. Mallarmé among other great poets was also forced once to edit a fashion magazine for the same reasons.)

I returned south. Came the harvest, the bull-fighting, the wine, followed by the morose period of storms and mists which heralded a premature winter. It was to be hard, according to the weather forecasts. So it proved to be. Once more I spent it alone with the owls – they uttered no complaints. There must have been plenty of stranded mice and bats in the old park with its tall trees. I was trying to write two books at once, and it wasn't the sort of thing one should try. Then came a summons from the Tibetans to share their New Year celebrations in early February. I had followed with interest the fortunes of this little monastery whose existence (now in financial danger) was due to the sudden influx of refugees after the fall of Tibet.[4] It was certainly the most interesting and forceful centre of Buddhism in France and the old chateau which had been made over to the order was ideally situated (by its remoteness among rather melancholy woods, not far from Autun) to the introspective studies and retreats and initiations which the Tibetan lamas promised a virgin audience of students. I had never so far been able to go – my travels had always drawn me out of France during the period when the Abbey was in full activity. But the link was firm – after all, the Kagu Ling clan had descended directly – by word of mouth, by breath to breath, by *bouche à la bouche*, of initiation – from the national poet of Tibet, Mila Repa, whose poems and teachings I had known since I was sixteen, and which summoned up for me at once the strange life I had lived in Darjiling, with its scripture classes, its Sunday School excursions to Tiger Hill (no tigers now!). Then, too, my father was curious and adventurous, and during the period while he looked after the tiny railway (Siliguri-Darjiling) he took us on many excursions, rides and walks in the wide Teesta valley. Once he went as far as Kalimpong, and often we were visitors to Buddhist monasteries when they were *en fête*. But from that early epoch onwards I had had no direct contact with things Tibetan. The little pamphlet came at a time when I was much in need of it – for my personal affairs were in disorder and I was plagued by a dozen different nagging contingencies. In spite of the weather – the whole of France was under snow and the long tally of snow damage and flood catastrophe completely filled the news bulletins – I decided to motor up in my little camping-car, hoping that if I went cautiously I could avoid trouble and arrive safely at my destination.

As usual, the reality seemed a good deal less dramatic than journalism suggested, though the autoroute was indeed swept by the wind and a dense thistle-swishing rain, with packets of visibility floating about, punctuated by white blackouts of sheer mist. One had the curious illusion that whole chunks of landscape were being shifted about by invisible scene-shifters, now advancing, now receding. At Lyon the usual smog-stained darkness set in as it always does, winter or summer. What ugliness, what 'urban growth'! Moreover what a fate to have overtaken the Mecca of gastronomy in France! Everyone dreads Lyon now, dipping into the great squat hollow in which the city lies – and on this beautiful arm of the river, too! It is no more a provincial capital but a suburb to end all suburbs. One comes out the other side with a sigh of relief – like a patient emerging from an anaesthetic. But its spirit is creeping down southwards and even my own little village is sending souls north to Lyon in search of work – hostages to the smog and smoke. In five years Sommières itself will be simply a dormitory for pale aspirin-ravaged city workers who wonder why they cannot sleep . . . North of Lyon the skies darkened and dense patches of fog called for headlights over long stretches; I had calculated on a landfall around five in the evening and I saw that I would not be far out in spite of these hazards which imposed caution and stealth.

The whole Maconnais seemed to be under water – the flooding of inland lakes had altered the prevailing topography in the most dramatic fashion. Just the tops of the tall poplars stood out above the water which had risen to their necks. In this way one could trace the course of major roads which had now disappeared. Pylons have been overturned like ninepins, electric wires trailed everywhere. The *Pompiers* and the army were out in force – transformed, for the emergency, into sailors, rescuing floating cattle or individuals marooned on their own rooftops. Fortunately the great parapets of the autoroute rode high above these water-ravaged valleys, and by the time I quitted it, the land was much higher and drying, though under deep snow. They were not very high, the hills I had to traverse to reach Autun, but they were high enough for snow. Yet mercifully the snowploughs had turned out, and a light thaw had set in to help them. One could see the holes in the tarmac sucked by the spring-thawing snow as it drained away into the valleys. It had turned very cold. I had entered a melancholy land with winding roads running through dense areas of forest thick with unburnt leaves and rotting loam. Farms were few and far between, traffic nil, petrol pumps far apart. I tanked up with some care, and lowered pressures on my little battle-wagon. When not fully loaded she tends to float off into the sky at the slightest excuse – particularly when there is high wind on the autoroutes. Now came Autun with its old-fashioned and solemn architecture and its pale population huddled into overcoats against the cutting wind which blew down upon them from the direction of Dijon. It is a market-town of some importance and rather beautiful in its cold way. The accent is somewhat sharp and rocky – it smells of the Dauphiné, of Grenoble. The people are brisk and brusque, indifferent to visitors, dreaming perhaps of selling up and moving south to where the sun shines. I traversed the old town and moved off into lowlands now – they formed a kind of pocket as if on a green billiard table, and cut off by a range of hills from the main body of France; down at the bottom of the pocket lay the remote chateau of Plaige in its cold woodlands. It took some finding. Hereabouts, too, there were streams which had jumped their banks, roads cut off, fallen trees and broken wires – but the road itself was clear, though by now night was signalled by fading light, and quite heavy snow was falling. It was appropriate, the snow; to rediscover the ambience of my childhood by any other element would have left something lacking. Moreover when, after coasting about among the white fields and asking my way of the occasional mortal I encountered in all the whiteness, I at last saw the tall prayer-masts of the chateau with their sodden drooping flags, I realized with a pleasant pang that the place the monks had been donated was itself a piece of old Nepal, of old Bhutan. It was precisely the sort of country-house-chateau which might be inhabited even today by a hill-Rajah. We had known some who lived in just such chateaux around Kuyseong and in the hills around Darjiling. Yet despite this tinge of Oriental appropriateness the old building still insisted, by its vast stables, hangars, *greniers*, that it was really an overgrown farm, and typical of the Norman north. I limped up towards it upon an execrable private road made viscous by the typical farm mud of the region, and after unearthing the monk in charge of the bookings signed the book and made myself known as a visitor for the weekend. There was some accommodation, and very pleasant too, in the well-heated chateau but I elected to sleep in my little car. I was used to it and liked the feeling of independence it conferred on me at night. So they allowed me to anchor it inside the walls of the grange, just outside the kitchen and refectory, an ideal strategic point. It was rather like being back at school again; dozens of people were arriving with every kind of transport and there seemed few who knew each other. Indeed it was very much like the first day of term at a public school. People floundered about, hunting down their accommodation, examining the premises, or else encountering friends last seen in India or Katmandu. The place was beautifully heated and the shrine room delightful. The hall notice-boards were sprinkled with announcements concerning the services to be held, and more urgent if more mundane appeals against taking muddy boots upstairs. The atmosphere was one of calm elation, that special joy when Dharma-crafting beings meet together. There were one or two also who had not broken the chain of tobacco as yet, and they hid themselves among the snowy trees in the park to take a last drag at a Gauloise Bleu. I was so grateful to the yoga which had liberated me (I used to be a heavy smoker) from this cruel addiction for some eight years now, without relapse. Dinner passed off with friendly animation and I made a couple of contacts, one a rather grim looking man with a long nose who looked as if he were an extreme sceptic. He did not actually say anything but his way of examining wall notices and looking round at his fellow diners (and sniffing) suggested that he was thinking to himself: 'This is all my eye and monkey's fur!' No need to say that the food was good; the French lamas must have cooked it for some of the dishes were very superior – cream of chestnuts was one. But I was tired after my long drive, and glad that I had opted for the privacy of the car where I could roll down my bed, light a candle for pleasure, read a few lines of Donne or Mila Repa before falling into a hushed sleep, dimly aware of movements about me in the darkness – for the dormitories in the barns were slowly filling up with sleeping-bag novices who had arrived after dark. The snow hushed and lulled all sharp sound. But the frost was heavy, and when I woke about three and crawled out to express myself in the snow, the sky was brilliant with stars – dagger-points of frosty light – and a chill crackling wind whirled down from the north bringing more snow. Incoherent and unpatterned memories and impressions of the past filled my mind. I was glad that it was snowing, for in my memories it always snowed and always the white fangs of the Himalayan Alps across the valley held the blue glass-glitter of ice all the year round. Plaige was like a small yet faithful miniature of those grandiose landscapes of my extreme youth – it was the stage version, so to speak, of an epic scenery.

In the evening, just before dinner, there had come the sound of some pretty smart drumming and crashing and I was told that the resident lamas – the dignitaries had not yet arrived to preside over the major ceremonies – practised a little in the evenings for the morning service. It is an unforgettable sound, this mixture of tooting and booming, of mice and elephants. It brought back so many forgotten impressions of the past – for this was the ordinary musical scheme of Nepal, Bhutan and all points north. It contrived to combine the sounds of an Alban Berg concerto with that of a goblin being castrated. But the noise did not last, it died away as the dinner gong sounded. Apparently the resident lamas enjoyed quarters on the third floor. Theirs was the music and the prayer which would draw us inexorably towards this galloping continuum – the natural force of the cosmos: the Tao!

Most everyone was up before dawn; I saw the kitchen lights switched on and heard the pop of the gas stove which manufactured strong tea for the visitors. I was glad of it, for it was mighty cold, and a heavy dew had turned into frost on my windscreen which I would have to scrape. I tried hot water but it froze as fast as I cleared it. The opening service was early also and the virtuous were already abroad, all creased and yellow and yawny from a night of icy sleep in the outbuildings. I was not going to miss the morning service for anything – I knew it would be full of memory-soliciting sounds and shapes. Irrationally I heard the voice of F saying: 'Our cosmology is a skandah short in their terms.' There was the smell of incense and muddy gumboots and milk on the stairs. The house was very warm and the friendly throne room as yet almost empty. It is pleasant to arrive a little early and prepare oneself by a quiet breathing and concentrating exercise. (There is nothing specially Tibetan about it: it is equally true for religious services in hallowed places consecrated to this kind of psychic activity, like cathedrals or Christian shrines. You have to make an effort if you want to suck out the marrow of things!)

Gradually the little chapel filled up, the doors were opened, the congregation took up its dispositions on the floor, many adopting the lotus pose. And then the gay body of lamas entered, their square humorous faces smiling, their tough square little bodies bustling forward with an irresistible momentum – the energy of mountain folk who have come to terms with cold and wind and who enjoy rude peasant health. The head lama was brimming with good nature and light and he took his routine in a competent and relaxed way. The youngest lama was a boy of twelve or so. It reminded me a little bit of a Greek Orthodox service where you are apt to come upon a couple of fine, if piratical-looking, old priests assisted by a dissolute-looking beadle and a shaky-looking adolescent who from time to time strikes a triangle and looks around with cretinous joy and astonishment. It was not quite that, for this little Tibetan was in charge of drums which would have rejoiced the heart of a jazz drummer. The chief lama paid the preliminary obeisances to various goddesses and gods of the various shrines. He walked round the altar, so to speak, bending down to croak a prayer, hardly audible, to the divinities, yet on a deep raucous note which reminded one of a tree frog at mating time. There was also something minatory about this serious survey – he was rather like a mastiff checking that all was well. You felt his scrupulous attention and awareness. Then he swept us with a glance and took his place and the service began. It is quite impossible to describe the pleasure and reassurance this ordinary little service gave me. The bongo drums and squiffy fifes brought it all back to me. It was like the plunging hooves of pack mules as they floundered on one of those narrow paths before falling into the ravines below. In a trice the rocky landscapes came into my mind. Always the question of height was the thing. The abysses were literally measureless for on those mountain paths the bandages of dense mist floated below as well as above you. Often one threw a boulder and stood waiting to see when, if ever, it would strike bottom. The waterless mountains of Nepal with their richly-oxygenated air and eternal snow-cloud shapes hiding secret monasteries – I could recover it all through this weird and tilting music. The drumming of hooves on rock! On those vertiginous paths, of course, mules frequently did go overboard – being such foolishly obstinate creatures. There was no room to manoeuvre so that the story was frequently told of them plunging over these precipices in a shower of stones. I had forgotten so many little things! I had forgotten just how physically dirty one could become for lack of water, living in a lamasery at ten thousand feet. Those sweetly enticing cloud-shape monasteries which look so good in photos were often pitiless and barren nooks good for nothing except contemplation and self-discovery through the altering of the mind's axis, through the art of breathing. At some point, in the stuffy intellectual attic of the quotidian mind a key clicked home, or a pane of glass was smashed, and the pure air rushed in to oxygenate the spirit of the contemplant. Water was as precious as it is in the waterless islands of the Aegean, and what was left over from the winter storms was kept for tea. Illness is comparatively rare up there in those fastnesses probably because though the lama's spiritual search is strenuous his daily life is anchored to a notion of living without tension, without stress – and the primal root of the disharmony which, in Taoist terms, sets off illness is precisely stress. I recalled all this while the service rolled on its way with the chanting and drumming; here and there in it, too, there occurred passages which sounded suddenly as if they were of Indian, even western, provenance. Graceful light airs which suggested Indian peasant songs, or even Scottish ballads; these only hovered for a moment and then returned back to the central gruffness of the two-tone melodic scheme, driven onward by the quavering trump of the bagpipes – squash a goose or a three-month baby slowly and you would get something like this hellish quaver. Then sizzle-bang-boom, the triangles and the big drum took over and the monks began their prostrations; some of them were young Frenchmen, and one hoped it was not just a romantic fad with them to learn Tibetan and turn Buddhist; or just a despairing backlash from the mental self-indulgence of Paris with its tedious mystagogues relentlessly complicating the obvious by giving it fancy names ... From Fraud to Freud and back again. Mind you, there would be much to excuse if this were actually the case. I know that if I were condemned to be a French intellectual of today I would certainly leap on the nearest mule and head for Lhasa. Slowly the service ran out of current like an electric train and, sliding down an inclined plane, came to rest on the pulse-beat of the bongo drum, while everyone relaxed and smiled round at his or her neighbour in congratulation; as if it had all been a huge success and entirely due to the wholesale cooperation of us all, which perhaps was really the case. It was breakfast time now, and everyone was thoroughly awake and good-humoured. One saw people more clearly, saw their natures and the roles they played in coming here for the Tibetan New Year. There were one or two very beautiful old ladies and some handsome young girls from Paris. There were also one or two silly-billies aged sixteen whose epithets began and ended with *vachement chouette* and who expressed the sort of excitement with the service that one might over a fine performance by a company of actors. Particularly the part of the service where the priest launches into a sort of marionette dance of the hands and wrists. Then there was an Australian who apparently found some special virtue in whirling a prayer-wheel as he ate – he looked like a mentally deficient potboy. 'You can buy electric ones now.' I told him. 'They run off a torch battery.' He looked at me with unfeigned disgust. I could almost hear him whisper to himself: 'Mechanized Buddhism! What next?' Later I saw him in the library immersed in a translation of the Mahamudra still absently twirling his propitiatory wheel. May a Tibetan demon fly away with him!

There was a very heavy frost and the milky light offered no promise of sun. Moreover trouble lay ahead for me – engine trouble. In cleaning up my little car, scraping off the ice and checking the heater, I realized that a vital part had worked loose and would have to be replaced or the thread would bite off. It was most vexatious; but if I left her there to freeze away to death I might have to wait for spring before I could move her! And the old chateau was miles from Autun where I might presume upon a technical sophistication to supply the missing part. I thought then that towards evening I would limp back along the road to Autun in the hope of mending the breach. It gave me the day for contacts and studies, and I used it to the full. The library was good and much in demand. There were a number of good lectures listed and almost continuous Tibetan classes with professors of whose proficiency one could have no doubt. The whole thing was organized effortlessly and well and clearly there was some master-brain behind the enterprise. But by late afternoon I felt it wiser to take advantage of the light and stalk back in all precariousness to Autun. This I did, and arrived only to find everything closed against the approaching weekend and the only decent garage in the place out of spares. They would have to be sent down from Paris, which would take a night; but with the coming strike on the railways . . . So went my Tibetan New Year. A draughty night in a cold hotel in Autun did nothing to assuage my irritation. Yet, in another sense, I felt that I had seen what I had come to see – the functioning of the abbey and the general state of instruction prevailing in it. The thing was serious. Tibet was here to stay, so to speak. I wondered if perhaps instead of going back to Kagu Ling as I had intended I should not head away down south; the weather reports were so uncompromisingly gloomy that my concern was pardonable.

Snow, ice, floods ... The spare did not arrive till late on Monday, and the car was not put right until Tuesday morn – by now the Tibetan dignitaries would have taken to the air like swans, heading back to India where the founder seminaries were situated. Yes, I would sneak home.

The autoroute was lashed with wind and rain, and the traffic on it – many heavy trailers, few private cars – set up chains of spray as if they had been heavy motor boats in a choppy sea. One good souse from their back wheels and one had to slow down and set the wipers to work at speed. And the wind swung me about like a pendulum. It was really hard and disagreeable driving and I felt half dead with fatigue. I thought I would climb off the autoroute and down into a valley but I did not want to land myself in a flood area so I waited until I saw the turn-off for Orange signalled; this part of the land I knew well, and it is rarely flooded. So it proved to be, and I felt that I might manage to rest my weary limbs in Avignon for a night before rolling back home across the *garrigues*. I knew that the Rhone was danger-high but had not jumped its banks as yet, and when I crossed it despite the flailing wind and rain (not to mention the invisible mountain snows melting into its sources and tributaries) it had not yet swallowed the islands, while the new bridge rode high and clear into town. But the town itself was sodden as a wet mattress, spectral, winter-locked. I don't know what put the Vaucluse fountain into my mind – but yes, I do. I saw an advertisement for some article of domestic ware called Vega – and my thoughts turned to a girl I had known under that starry name. The star on the advertisement reminded me of the intense bright blue – almost sapphire – of her eyes. Vega, pole star of the ancients, had always been my favourite fixed star. How often I have lain on the deck of a caique or a liner in the Aegean watching that marvellous gem-like stare, unwinking, unmoving, all-seeing. The girl had some of this in her own steady regard – the uncompromising brightnes of a cat's eyes, a Persian kitten, say. When she was interested in something or someone she sat so still that she didn't seem to be breathing, she could have been dead, fixing you with these 'blue lamps of heaven' – let us indulge her memory with a seventeenth-century conceit from Darley. But here in Avignon on that rainy afternoon I suddenly thought of her and wondered if I should not lie that night in the little hotel we knew once by the roaring waters of Petrarchian Vaucluse. She too had been a Taoist with the requisite look of melting mischief as required by the recipe of Chang. I had first come under this disquieting gaze in Geneva. A little group of psychiatrists – all Jungians – had asked if they could meet me and ask a few questions. I think they were just curious to size me up and see if I was quite right in the head. It was not the first time that such a thing had come about. They were friends of other friends, and so I agreed and we met in the rather pleasant brasserie and beer-hall – a chop-house, really – called Bovard which should have been 'classé' and which has now been swept away and turned into a bank. Anyway in the background there sat Vega staring at me – looking right through me, as if she could count all the small change in my pocket. And the conversation was lively and full of pith. I gathered that she was the wife or mistress of one of the doctors present though I could not decide which one. Nevertheless, the evening came to an end and off we all went home. A fortnight later I ran into her in Bounyon where I was trying to buy a cheese called Vacherin. I had forgotten her, actually, and she had to jog my memory by references to this pleasant but most unmemorable evening. We went to have a coffee together and it was here in a shady café that I started to get to know Vega. To cut a long story short in the midst of a thousand trivia she said that she was a real old-fashioned reader. Every year she chose one author and read everything about him. She added that this year the lucky author was Nietzsche and she was in mid-channel. Why did this remark make an instant impression on me? Because I myself had been doing more or less the same sort of thing – an echo of it, so to speak. I had been collecting and sifting information about Lou Andrée Salome with the vague notion of writing an essay on this remarkable and gifted enchantress, who as a young girl bewitched Nietzsche, then had a child by Rilke and ended up in old age as Freud's most deeply cherished pupil and friend. How extra-ordinary that none of her many books, including the capital essays on Nietzsche and Rilke, were available in English! Actually my project was hopeless, I knew, because of my lack of German. Nevertheless this strange frieze of characters gave me food for thought; I had planned to press the story of their lives forward as far as the lake of Orta, which I was then proposing to visit. It was here that the thirty-year-old philosopher proposed to the eighteen-year-old girl, it was here that he outlined the whole scenario of Zarathustra! Once one has read of the notebooks in which they played question-and-answer games and riddles based on philo-sophic questions it seems quite possible that passages of the great classic could actually have been written by her. The idea, however far-fetched, intrigued me. And with this end in mind I obtained a commission from an American paper to write a vignette on the Borromean Islands which lay hard by on the larger lake, Maggiori. 'How odd!' I said, and she echoed me, 'Why odd?' I said that I was doing the same sort of thing and added, 'I am going down to Orta next Sunday for a week. I want to see the little lake where they were so happy when they were young. I have some notions about her making a contribution to Zarathustra – which I shall never be able to check because I have no German.'

'Orta?' She was looking at me very strangely indeed; then she started to laugh. 'Look,' she said, 'I have just come from the station.' And extracting from her bag a railway reservation she placed it before me on the table. I saw it was a return ticket to Stresa which I knew was, so to speak, the railhead for the lake of Orta. The date was for the following weekend! The coincidence was unbelievable, and we both laughed.

'I wanted to visit the little sacred hill with all the chapels to try and see which was the one in which he proposed to her only to be rejected – quite properly; he was not fit to be married to a woman and she would have made a wretched wife, always on the move, always disappearing.'

'The Monte Sacro?'

'Yes. I have never been.'

'Nor have I.'

I produced a travel brochure with some pictures of the lake, and she produced an identical one.

'But your ticket is a single – are you alone?'

'Yes.'

'Then can we meet? Shall we meet?'

'Of course. I will bring the books I have.'

'Yes, so shall I.'

It was one of these strange encounters which are all too rare in life and which make it echo. We shook hands rather awkwardly as we said goodbye; the blue regard set up a memory in me of some half-forgotten poem which mentioned the 'vernal twinkling of butterflies' in Coleridge – I had tried in vain to trace the quotation; nor could I now remember who had written the poem. All I remembered of the blonde girl now was the blue regard of a fixed star, staring down from mid-heaven upon the smooth lake. In my absent-minded way I had forgotten even to write down her name and phone number – in case of any change of plan. It was better perhaps. It gave her a kind of anonymity. I motored back to Provence during the night to collect my affairs and make my dispositions for Italy. I did not intend to rush it, and in my little camper I could easily make Novarra in one day; I would dawdle, I thought, round Maggiori and landfall at The Dragon in Orta well before Saturday. Then I would meet her train at Stresa – though she did not know this as yet!

V

So it fell out. I crossed the wide plain of Novarra one late afternoon; all the
corn had caught alight on both sides of the road and a racing fire seemed to
stretch away to the horizon on either side of me. It was a dramatic vision of
destruction! But it was so very hot that I did not linger but raced through,
fearing an exploding petrol tank or some such mishap. After a very few
more kilometres the green Alpine meadows and foothills started to rise
ahead of me and suddenly it was there – a modest green signpost directing
me to the tiny kidney-shaped lake I was hunting for: Nietzsche's Orta.
('Our Orta' he had written in a love letter to Lou.) The approaches grew
narrower, more sinuous, and densely wooded – nightingales sang everywhere, just as they do in Provence. The lake came up, as if presented upon
the palm of an invisible conjuror's hand, and upon it the sacred island with
its monastery and tall trees, all so toy-like and so calm and so small and so
homely in scale. The green lake edge was Irish green. As for Orta, Balzac
described it once with a simile that I had thought suspect, as altogether too
plump, 'a pearl in a green jewel case' ... Quite the contrary. It is not. He
was stirred by the strange opalescent quality of the light and the
translucent shifts of colour on the mountains which cradled and framed
the island. This hazy misty feeling throws everything in and out of focus
and gives a feeling of unreality, or iridescence, to the whole waterscape.
Moreover, the whole thing is double for when the water is calm the
mountains repeat themselves in it and one does not know which side up
one is; you have the feeling sometimes of walking on the sky. No, Balzac's
image is very exact, and cannot be bettered.

I rolled down these shadowy inclines, round a dozen curves, and came
to rest in the tiny square with its two inns, its pleasant arcades and small
cafés. The Dragon was a pleasant little *auberge* as well with its rooms
opening on the lake. Vega was to lodge at the Castello opposite, twenty

yards away. We would be able to wave from our respective balconies over the water! I would have liked to send flowers to her room but I did not have her name, like the fool I was. I went however and consulted the visitors' book – a very vague document kept in pencil by a near-analphabetic – in the hope of discovering it, since she said she had booked there. I supposed that she was German by marriage though I knew her to be French by birth. Which name then? There was only one person expected for the next evening and she was called Chantal De Legume. My heart sank. Just the thought that she might be called Chantal De Legume made me burst into a sweat of apprehension. It would spoil everything – such a name comprised everything! I know it is irrational but I hoped desperately that she was not called Chantal De Legume. (She is *not* called Chantal De Legume!)

I renounced the flowers, and took a boat to drift on that quiet water for an hour or so before dinner time, reflecting idly on that long-lost philosopher whose name nobody in Orta would know today – except perhaps the *curé* (and then only as an anti-Christ). The old man who rowed me about was calm and polite but not voluble; his father would have been of an age to ferry Nietzsche and Lou out upon the waters of Orta, to take them to the island of San Julio; or perhaps his grandfather? But no, for Lou lived on until the beginning of the Nazi epoch in Germany. I could actually have met her. The water was so warm that I knew I should be tempted to take a silent night-swim in it later on. I had brought my own little Zodiac dinghy with its motor, but Orta is too small a lake to poison with outboard motors. It is made for the slow sweep of oars, the slow creak of wood not properly imbibed by a winter of submersion. The little awnings and the gay frills of the boat were rather dusty and damp. Summer was not yet here. High above me as I lay in the sheets of the boat rose the Monte Sacro – I could see St Francis hanging off a wooded balcony and waving to me. I waved back but I wanted to save him until Vega came. The twenty little chapels – each as big as a Swiss chalet – house twenty *tableaux* – scenes from the life of St Francis – enacted by life-size statues in *gutta percha*, appropriately dressed and painted, each different, and all grandiose. Vega was sure that Nietzsche, being a man, would have sought the aid of one such shrine when he proposed to Lou! (For a great man he was extraordinarily timid.) The problem was which one – she had come here to find that out. But I had other fish to fry – for I had been reading Nietzsche and discovering what had really been ailing him here in Orta, the gestation of his critical books in which he declared war on Christianity in the name of Heraclitus and

44

the ancient Greeks. His target was no less than the Christian god, God
the Father.

Night fell, the mists closed in and filtered eerily among the mossy vege-
tation, trailing long tentacles; the lake began to creep about, as it were, for
such was the illusion given by moving mists and waters forever rubbing
out and correcting images of sky and mountain. The sky full of stars
burned furiously in the water, broken up by belfries and cupolas and the
slow planetary trails carved by the boats (now lit like fireflies) as they
crawled about the lake. Never have I experienced such a sense of peace,
suspended upon a narrow balcony between sky, mountain and
water – feeling as if I myself had become a trail of vapour slowly shifting
about at the behest of a current of wind, of water. The sky turned slowly
through its arc as if projected by a stage diorama. Time filled the heart
like an hour-glass. I had an early dinner and turned in, though for a long
moment before sleeping I watched the shifting spectacle offered by the
polished water outside the balcony window. I wondered whether Vega
would find what she was seeking – the chapel where the timid but
brilliant (though neurotic: all those migraines!) professor plucked up his
courage to propose not marriage but ... concubinage to the slim and
graceful Slav whose brilliance he so admired. And then, the tragic enigma
posed by his collapse into mania; surely Lou in her old age must have seen
the rationale of the whole thing through the lens of Freudian theory – it
still holds firm. The old sage Freud considered her one of his most brilliant pupils. He addresses her, in a letter, as 'My indomitable friend'. He
was no Zarathustra either, though he preserved his inquisitorial sanity to
the end. As for Nietzsche, it was war to the knife against three fathers –
or rather against God the Father (the Christian God), God the Son (his
own father and all he stood for in the realm of ideas) – he never forgot
hearing his mother hiss at him: 'You are a reproach to your father's
grave'; the words had bitten deep into his sensibility – and then God the
Holy Ghost, was Wagner of course, whom he also had to deny and
destroy. Was it not the shock of this tremendous struggle that overturned
his reason? Sometimes when he was mad he spoke of Cosima Wagner.
'My lady Cosima sent me here ... ' Of course in the turbulence of his
broken mind the wife of the Holy Ghost must have been a highly desirable muse in the Oedipus context! And finally, of course, Mother won
out, his own earthly mother; triumphantly she gathered all this human
wreckage into her arms, while the sister quietly betrayed him by falsifying
the text of his work with anti-Jewish interpolations ... What a fate, what
a man, what a place! I fell asleep thinking of the little chapels on the

wooden hill above me. Next day was clear, but by evening a thick mist came down, and this time in a definitive manner – you could not see your hand before your face. My heart sank. Stresa was only a quarter of an hour's drive – I knew the way by heart. But never have I seen such dense fog. The hotel proprietor told me curtly that it would not lift until morning; I stood no chance of climbing out of the hollow where Orta lies so I had better give up the notion of driving to the station and stay put. It enraged me. I closed my eyes at the dinner table and mentally rememorized every inch of the road round the lake – I had done it several times now. It was extremely foolhardy, I knew, but I thought I would try and get up on to the main road, travelling blind. I got pitying looks from everyone. They said that after a hundred yards I should be forced to leave the car and walk back to the hotel. Nevertheless I set off. It was terrifying, I could not even see my own headlights; I was travelling by memory purely, as if in a dream. I was guided by the strip of cobbling on the side of the road, the vibration it made on my tyres. But the gods heard my prayers. Suddenly, like a veil snatched away, the whole fog was peeled back to reveal a bright pure sky with ardent stars and with Vega overhead giving me the fixed-star look – almost turquoise this time. I shouted with joy and put on speed, to arrive in Stresa with an hour to spare which I happily spent in the empty buffet, reading.

How eerie her arrival was; a light and wholly irrational snowstorm of light flakes had started. The snow melted as it touched ground. You could hear the train far away in the darkness somewhere, the mesh of wheels and its little apologetic foghorn. An answering bell somewhere in the station started to echo, started to throb. Then in the further darkness of the hinterland, upon the velvety screen of night, as if in response I saw a sudden line of yellow lights moving slowly across the skyline, softly tinkling as the whole chaplet came slowly and sinuously down to the level of the plain. The little station bell went mad now. It throbbed as if it had a high temperture. I waited on the dark platform with this very light snow – a mere swish-like spray – caressing my neck. The train arrived with a clamour and a final sprint, a rush. It came to rest in the station; it was apparently empty. There was not even a guard aboard. In my disappointment I was about to turn away and set off back to Orta when at the very end a carriage door opened, a bar of light fell on the snowy platform, and Vega stepped out. She stood there smiling with the snow on her furs, on her blonde head, a little hesitant and questioning, but with the firm blue regard of happiness. Enfin! I ran forward, seized her bag and led her back to the car. She had not expected to be met and so was a little pleased and confused.

The memory of those few days – the smooth lake at night, the polished mountains and the vernal hills where the nightingales sang night and day – has become a fused up continuum where the details have all melted into one overwhelming impression of divine attachment and friendship. The little chapels we explored were so extraordinary and so various, the hills so green, the wine so good, our hosts so tender and welcoming. There was nothing to mar the felicity of this intellectual adventure – not a false note or a false sentiment to break or bruise this calm and content, as of brother and sister meeting by the lake of Zarathustra. We recognized each other through Nietzsche and Lou, sharing like them an attachment which was as ardent as it was limpid. When it was time to part she said, somewhat maliciously, 'Shall I sign all my letters Chantal De Legume so that you can identify me?' But I had already mentally allocated to her the name of my protecting star, for her eyes were of the same fine colour. Vega it should be. All this came suddenly back to me now as I negotiated the green fields and sodden meadows of Montfavet and l'Isle-sur-Sorgue. I compiled those ancient memories with happiness and reserve, remembering also the long silences we shared, swimming at night in the lake. Once she went for a long walk alone. Our documents littered the floor of her room. I had brought photostats of the thunderous handwriting of Nietzsche's letters to Strindberg, the mad declarations of his Godship. At night, late at night, the smoke of candles which had long expired drifted over our arguments and filled the room, with its high ceilings decorated by plaster nymphs and scrolls. She slept with her face on her arm and I watched her sleep, so contentedly, so thoroughly. She had found the chapel that she sought – but who would ever be able to prove her contention that it was here in Number 14 that Nietzsche had taken Lou's hand in his and asked her to live with him? And why did Lou refuse? We will, I presume, never know the truth, for she has not deigned to tell us. But she was a fiery Slav and he was, after all, a timid German professor condemned by his health to premature retirement. And he lacked humour. What he sought for himself – he had recognized full well that Heraclitus and the early Greeks held the key he so frantically sought – was simply The Look, the equable look of the Tao which contains the salt of humour and complicity and irony in its depths. 'Nobody trusts art any more,' said Vega sadly.

So the time came to part and I made my slow way home across the midriff of Italy, camping a night on the way in order to savour the delight and simplicity of this prime event. It was not the last; whenever I got a telegram signed Vega it offered me a landfall somewhere in Europe which concerned her steady search for the essence of Nietzsche's thought. I got used to crossing Europe, slithering back and forth across the map, with the delightful knowledge that just for a few hours or a few days I would see her again. Meanwhile we exchanged books and documents and photos of our two subjects, Wagner and Cosima. And she introduced me to the marvellously sensitive trilogy of musical studies by Guy De Portalès – why isn't his *Nietzsche en Italie* still available among the paperbacks? It's a shame! And so at last we came to the end of our search and to say farewell we came here, to the Fontaine De Vaucluse. The years passed. We still met in this strange unbroken intimacy in far-away places – Salzburg, Silz Maria, Eze. But Orta had marked us both and it would be long before we managed to disentangle Nietzsche from our mental lives. Vega visited Russia, and then Greece, and though I was not there to show her round, friend Nietzsche was, and he did her the honours. The visit opened up another magic casement in the pre-Socratics, notably on Heraclitus and Empedocles about whom he had projected a book. Alas! only the notes he made for it remain to us, with here and there a typical thunderflash of thought which shows us in which direction it might have gone. On Empedocles he says: 'He looked for Art and only found science. *Science creates Fausts*!' She now fully understood and approved my interpretation of Zarathustra's struggle as well as the pity of his failure to grasp the Heraclitean quiddity; he saw it, he reached out his hand to grasp it, but . . . His art remained. But art is a second-best, however great, and he knew this now when it was too late! With him a whole epoch nose-dives into the bottomless pit of matter and is lost. It was in Orta that despite Lou's kind and tender refusal, Nietzsche was able to swallow his mortification and go on to outline his coming work to her – including the theory of 'eternal recurrence' which he claimed to have developed upon an ancient Greek basis. What he sought however was much more like an eternal simultaneity – the continuous eternal and simultaneous presence of everything mortal or material or in essence, wrapped into a package with all Time included in it – and the whole of it present in every thought, in every drawn breath, an incandescent Now!

Our visit to the country of Petrarch was more fortuitous though Vega was after all an Avignon girl with relations in the town whom she wished to see before going on a long journey which would take her far from France for several years. Happily, I lived so close by that I was able to profit from this descent into the Vaucluse, and we spent some time travelling together to the smaller villages, the more evocative corners of Provence. I personally would not have risked such a tourist spot as the fountain of Vaucluse but she insisted, and the trip as it turned out was delightful; it was in mid-winter. There was not a soul – not even the ghost of Laura rising from the foam. Was it Vega's local patriotism that made her put up such an effective *plaidoyer* for Petrarch? I had been rather inclined to see in him one of the cry-babies of love-poetry. But thanks to her I now saw beneath the trappings of romance and realized him as the great and deeply responsible humanist, fully aware that he had stirred a whole culture to its roots and struck chords deeper than any poet before him. She rounded out the portrait in some detail – the courtier, the diplomat, the dispirited lover of another's wife. Then all the sudden excursions into the neighbouring countries, followed always by a retreat to this sunless ravine where he could polish his verses to the rushing of the waters. The great poem on Africa, and the essay on solitude, the passion for St Augustine . . . I had no idea he was an artist of such stature – I owe the knowledge to Vega. Moreover, it was due to her that I hunted down texts of his little autobiographical dialogues entitled *Secretum Meum* as well as the touching and poetic statements in *De Vita Solitaria* in which he deals with the heralidic solitude of the artist. This last document was sent to me some months later from Geneva as a Christmas present. It was beautifully bound in scarlet vellum – a fitting setting for a great poet's confession.

Well, all this was in the past now, but my memories of these episodes were still fresh, and the time of day I had chosen to descend on the sacred fountain was appropriate to the theme of my reflections. Moreover it was snowing, and heavily snowing at that. Ice crunched under my wheels. The villagers were shuttered and huddled upon themselves with only plumes of smoke from cottage chimneys to suggest human habitation. I could hear the roar of the distant fountain as it crashed out of the rock-face into the great circular pool where it lashed and writhed, for all the world as if it were boiling hot. The town was in darkness save for a glim here and there; one point of light shone from the little hotel where we had once stayed. I laid the car up in the snowy park and with my nose well tucked into my scarf ran down the pathways by the racing river to the glassfronted door of the place where I knocked once or twice rather sharply, in order to be heard above the roaring water. The madam of the establishment who was busy somewhere in the depths came short-sightedly towards me with a torch. Who could it be at such a time, on such a night? She did not at first recognize me but, good trusting soul, came towards me to parley through the glass door. It did not take long to recall who I was and she let me into the bar where I drank a welcome hot grog while she sat and kept me company. The place had not yet opened for the tourist season but she had come over for the weekend to test the heating and water systems; and indeed the heating was on and the whole place cosy. She offered to lodge me for the night but I preferred to sleep high up by the fountain in my little camper; but I would not say no to a sandwich. 'A sandwich!' she cried indignantly. 'You shall dine properly in my hotel.' It did not take long to prepare; she served me a trout with almonds – the trout grows *à domicile* here – followed by a good cheese with a bottle of Côte de Ventoux. And while I ate she came to talk to me in her kind and desultory fashion. Where was the blond lady, she wanted to know? She was in Africa. 'Once after your visit she came back here alone.' I knew this for Vega had written to me from here, and in the same sort of season, for she described the heavy snow falling and being smoothed away in the racing waters – and then an unusual touch which I had just come upon myself; the great trout were rising to the snowflakes and taking them as if they were bait! 'A strange place to bring an unhealed love-affair.' That was how she had once put it, referring to Petrarch. After dinner I ploughed my way up into the ravine as far as the macadam goes, and then turned off with my nose to the cliff to doss down. The intense white glare of the snow reflected so much light that one had the illusion that there was still a lingering twilight. The roar of the water was deafening; it was like being in the engine-room of some great ship, sleeping between the pulsing sweating turbines as they drove one rushing through the sea. What a lapidary's wheel on which to polish the first elegiac poems of an entire epoch! One's whole consciousness was quite engulfed in this steady drumming – as if upon a heavy vellum drumhead. The snow was falling in great meshes and wreaths and chaplets, and the water was swirling and polishing the black cliffs as it streaked for the sea. The river hereabouts is too fast for the fish, but a little lower down it is dark and pithy with trout. I made up my bed, heated up and then switched prudently off before turning in. It was wonderfully healing, the boom of the river – the dense cocoon of sound swaddled every nerve. Old conversations came back to mind, lazily, as if projected upon the darkness, wrestling with the desire to sleep.

'And Laura, was she real?'

'Does it matter?'

'Yes and no.'

'If invented she was still as real as any of his readers – as you or I are.'

'And if real she was only the ghost of an echo of a mood. In the book she dies, remember?'

'Africa! Sitting here in this roaring nautilus of sound he dreamed of Africa and read St Augustine.'

'And so for Laura there were many candidates for the part.'

'What names! What beauties!'

'Laura di Audiberto [Hugo de Sade's wife], Laura di Sabran, Laura di Chiabu, Laura Colonna ... '

'An all-star cast.'

'All star-crossed women.'

'The Happy Few rather.'

Or are human beings just recordings made by some terrifying voice from elsewhere?

In my half-sleep I was reminded of a story by Queba the Lebanese in which a famous writer manages to project his heroine to such good effect that the public believes her to be based on some real woman. Scents are named after her, and streets, and newborn children. But the author himself has never been seen out with a woman. Always alone. Scenting a story, in the manner of journalists, a woman editor asks her newspaper to announce a ballot – the public must vote for a real or imagined original for the famous heroine. They vote overwhelmingly in favour of an imagined heroine. The author is beside himself with anxiety and sorrow. 'She is not real enough, then, and she will never arrive.' So he goes home in despair and takes his own life, having at last realized the truth. Of his last story nothing remains save the enigmatic title it was to bear, *Death Has Blue Eyes*.

The water went on, rubbing and polishing its own echoes, drumming upon the darkness, upon the soft wadded walls lining the convolutions of some marvellous sea-shell. The thread which I held in my fingers I had first picked up – the clue, the inkling – from the great stone Gorgon in the island of Corfu – her cartoon of gay madness, ecstasy, hypomania – call it what you will. The clues led steadily on, and upon them I had threaded these experiences, all related and all congruent to a poetic life and practice. Where would it next lead me? I did not know, I did not care. Somewhere in Africa Vega would be writing me a letter, probably reproaching me for some un-Roman weakness, for she was a girl who did not spare her friends. I had written, saying: 'I am beginning to feel like some very old and moulting penguin left upon a small and rapidly melting ice-floe – call it European culture. Lord God, send the bomb, I sometimes cry! Then I think of vega, and, with a gesture, I stay the blow! Not yet, for Vega lives!' In her last letter – so many months ago – she enclosed the French text of a Chinese poem called 'Woman' which I Englished for

a friend in the following manner. She did not say where she got it, and I
have hunted in every likely place and asked my friends to hunt in Paris. I
apologize if I have broached a copyright.

WOMAN

How sad it is to be a woman!
Nothing on earth is held so cheap;
When boys stand leaning at the sill,
Like Gods tumbled out of Heaven.
Their hearts compass the Four Oceans,
The dust and the wind of a thousand thousand miles.
But no one is glad when a girl is born –
By her the family sets no store.
When she grows up she hides in her room
Scared to look a man in the face.
Nobody cries when she leaves her home, save she.
As suddenly as clouds when rain pauses,
She bows her head, composes her face, her teeth
Are pressed into her red lips, she bows and kneels
O! countless times. She must humble herself even to servants.
His love is as distant as a star,
Yet always the sunflower turns towards the sun.
Her heart is more sundered than water from fire,
A hundred ills are heaped on her; her face will follow
The changes of the years, will wear its age.
Her Lord will find new treasures.
They that were once like substance and shadow
Are now as distant as Hu from Ch'in [two places]
Or as Ts'an is from Ch'en [two stars].

3rd Century. Chinese

How odd that these apparently disparate incidents were all held together
in my mind by a slender chain of echoes, a predisposition which stretched
back to my twenty-third year in the remote (then) island of Corfu where I
had taken up residence with the intention of trying my hand at being a
poet – or at least a writer of some sort. It seemed clear now, as I thought
back to that prehistoric time, that the main inhibition against giving
Chang's book a conventional review (what I had promised) was the
echoes it had set off in my memory. I could not bring a coolly critical
intelligence to bear on his text. This sense of indecision had been helped
by the fact that I had also been trying to compile some sketchy

52

autobiographical notes for an American friend who was anxious to trace what he called 'the inner autobiography' of my poetry. It dawned on me in answering his letters that the central preoccupation of the then unfledged young poet of Corfu had been always somehow linked with childhood dreams of Tibet which had at last concretized themselves about the Tao – the great poem of Lao Tsu. In the *Black Book*, written around 1936, I find a Tibetan epigraph. The novel was published in 1938, the year before the war; already my first poems were gathered into a bouquet to present to this *amor fati* from Lhasa, the tantric dakini who had guided and inspired me. It was a life sentence and it helped me to put a calm face upon the despair of the war years with their wanton murders of time and talent and truth. When the war came I had just turned twenty-seven. Among my papers, long after it had ended, I found a forgotten article I had contributed to the *Aryan Path*, called 'Tao and Its Glozes'. The old *Aryan Path*, published from 51 Mahatma Gandhi Road, Bombay, was even then the most distinguished journal of the day devoted to theosophy, and my amateur article was published as a sort of little preface to the issue of December 1939, by which time my island life had ended and I was adrift in Athens waiting upon fate, waiting upon the Axis.

I reprint it here for old times' sake, and also as evidence of my constant attachment to the principle of non-attachment as outlined in the poem! It was not a bad way to greet a world war. I note also the use of the adjective 'heraldic' for which I have often had to answer the critics. It means simply the 'mandala' of the poet or of the poem. It is the alchemical sigil or signature of the individual; what's left with the ego extracted. It is the pure nonentity of the entity for which the poem stands like an ideogram! It sounds rather enigmatic put like that, though in fact it boils down simply to the crucial smile which I exchanged with Chang over the kitchen sink, and which needs no gloze. Language confronts this sort of reality with despair which rapidly turns to humour and, in the face of earnest or too earnest questioners, to slapstick. Another way of going about it would be to look up the Saxon word 'ullage' in the dictionary; the definition of it – 'what a cask wants of being full' – will exercise your reason to the snapping point – especially if your cask contains wine! It is another sort of koan – or can be used as one! The war was a time of hesitant stock-taking for all of us, and my little article with all its solemnity and youthful lack of experience – not to mention its inexactitudes – was a humble attempt to greet it with an act of affirmation. It may be a bit boring to read now, but for the young man in question it was a capital document.

TAO AND ITS GLOZES

(Lawrence Durrell in the following article suggests a method whereby the real Tao can be differentiated from that which is not the Tao. He rightly perceives that Tao is a philosophy, but also much more. Indeed it is 'the uncreate unborn and eternal energy of nature, manifesting periodically. Nature as well as man when it reaches purity will reach rest, and then all become one with Tao, which is the source of all bliss and felicity. As in the Hindu and Buddhistic philosophies, such purity and bliss and immortality can only be reached through the exercise of virtue and perfect quietude of our worldly spirit; the human mind has to control and finally subdue and even crush the turbulent action of man's physical nature; and the sooner he reaches the required degree of moral purification, the happier he will feel.' – EDS)

It has become a commonplace in literary criticism today to refer to the disparities which exist between certain portions of Lao Tsu's *Book of the Simple Way*: to accept, with the limpid resignation of the scholar, the apparent confusions (the word is repeatedly used) of which the text seems so full. So far, it seems, no one has tried to disentangle the conflicting fibres of doctrine and statement. Indeed, the task is not one to attract the boldest of textual scholars, for properly speaking no text exists which would offer the reader any canon on which to build an analytical or critical scheme. Yet it seems to me that a method may be found – perhaps not stable or exhaustive enough to satisfy the pedant, but sufficiently exciting to interest the student of Tao – a method by which one may catch glimpses of the original work among the glozes and shifting emendations of later scribes. The clue lies embedded like a diamond in the body of the text itself; a clue sufficiently cardinal to allow one a firm working foundation.

Now Tao has been defined as a philosophy which remains always in sharp contradistinction to the Confucian (more generally the 'Socratic') dialect of the ethic; but it is more than that. (The word 'Philosophy' still carries with it the taint of method given it by the Greeks, from which it has been imposible to free it.) It is an attempt to localize an experience, which itself is too comprehensive to be included in the mere confines of language. Throughout the book one can feel the language probing, like a pair of giant callipers, attempting to circumscribe a realm, for the expression of which we have nothing between the madman's idiom and the A minor Quartet. The searchlight of the ratiocinative principle is too weak to light up this territory: words themselves are used as a kind of sculpture, to symbolize what cannot be directly expressed: the heraldry of language is called into play to accentuate, to attest to, to pierce through the rind of the merely cognative impulse and delineate once and for all the mystery, the resting place of the Tao.

'The true Tao is not the subject of discussion.' In your opening statement you are faced with an attitude which, more exactly expressed as the text proceeds, ends in a complete and final denial of principle; a denial, in fact, of polarity, of schism. The affirmation here is that of a total personality, speaking from its totality. In the symbol of the Simple Way, expressed once and for all, you will find no trace of that abruption of the personality from its cosmos which has hallucinated European thought ever since pre-Socratic times. There is, to write nicely, no human entity; it is merged in the All. Here there is no trace of the rupture between the individual and his scenery. Fused, there remains only the gigantic landscape of the spirit, in which our Aryan problem ('To be, or not to be') is swallowed up, exhausted, sucked dry by the eternal factor – the Tao. The house admits its resident: the tenant is absorbed, like a piece of tissue, into the very walls of his spiritual house. The world of the definition is exploded. All this is so exhaustively written out in the book that it seems a little difficult at first to locate those areas in which the conflicting ideas enter. But with this profound clue (the denial, the absolution of principle) it would seem possible to retrace one's steps; and against this rule, measure the various phases of the text.

One thing becomes clear: if the denial of the dogmatic principle is the key-note of the document, then what confusions there are operate always in the realm of the *ethic*. It is only here that the voice becomes muffled, that the statement, otherwise so pure in its lingual evasions of the rule, becomes muddy, ambiguous.

The struggle is directed always against the Confucian scheme, the precocious assumption of man over men, over God, over t: e spiritual landscape; and luckily for us the Confucian contribution serves admirably to light up for us those precise departments of the idea which might remain as yet obscure.

> When a man with a taste for reforming the
> world takes the business in hand, it
> is easily seen that there is no end to it.
> For spiritual vessels are not fashioned in
> the world. Whoever makes, destroys;
> whoever grasps, loses.

And again:

> A sage is one who is full of rectitude,
> but he does not, on that account, hack and
> carve at others ... He is upright and yet
> does not undertake to straighten others.

In these two extracts from Lao Tsu his stance seems clearly enough defined. He refuses the dogma with its sharp black and white tones. Within the experience of which he talks there is room for infinite adjustment, infinite movement. The imposition of the iron scheme is a violence from which he utterly dissociates himself; his method is a wingless flying – an act which operates along a line where the mere mechanics of the act is lost; is irrelevant. His refusal to *transform* the flora and fauna of his world is a direct challenge to the world of dogmatic relations, where good is balanced against evil, black against white, being against non-being; the world of opposites, from which alone flowers the ethic, the canon, the principle. In his refusal to accept the limited concepts of language, he shows his wariness against the destroying, limiting effect of definition.

> It is when we come to speak of Beauty as a thing
> apart that we at once define Ugliness. So
> when goodness is seen to be good, then we
> become aware of what is evil ... For this
> reason the Sage only concerns himself with
> that which does not give rise to prejudice.

He will not place himself at the mercy of the dogmatic principle, which, he realizes, can carry embedded in it the poisons of the divided personality, against which the volatile principle of *being* is at war. Consequently he sees that the ratiocinative principle *itself* must go; and as the document closes, this is the note which is sounded in a last exhaustion; the last attempt to speak coherently from the very heart of Tao.

If we accept this as the ultimate statement from which the Tao lives, then it at once becomes obvious that we have in our hands a clue which relates to the actual text. For it is precisely where there occur abrupt expressions of dogma that the same 'confusions' also arise of which our scholars have talked for so long.

But let us pause for a moment to consider those to whom we owe the impurities in the text. What concerned *them* was never the Tao itself (the inexpressible IT): but merely a means of realizing it, tapping reservoirs for Peace; transforming it into an ideal easily attainable by religious *practice*. The history of this book: the subsequent erection of a huge and corrupt dogmatic theology around it – these prove our point beyond all doubt. What concerned the men who came after was a *practice* of Tao – a thing which could never exist in something whose theme was merely the localization of The Experience, with which language could deal, at the best, imprecisely. Their concern was credo; a credo that carried with it the iron imperative.

If we go back, then, keeping this fact in mind, we at once fall upon passages which carry the strange theological imperatives bedded in them.

> The pride of wealth and glory is companied
> with care, so that *one should come to a full
> stop* when a good work is completed, and when
> honour is advancing.

The imperative here is barbed with implications; the theological overtone slightly too obvious.

> By expelling impure things from the mind
> it is possible to remain untainted and to
> continue in obscurity . . .

Quotation in bulk would be tiresome. The object of this note, impertinent enough in itself, is not to provide a hunting ground for the contentious scholar; rather I have suggested an exciting game which would interest those for whom the *Book of the Simple Way* is still confused, still a little obscure. By striking at the ethic wherever it appears in the text, one is suddenly faced with a genuine clearance of all the 'confusions'. The book is empty of dead wood, the tree itself stands out, free and glowing, as it must have been originally.

Empty the document of these bewildering *volte-faces* and the circle finds itself harmoniously closed once more; we enter the centrum again. The 'confusions' have gone.

*　　*　　*

Have the 'confusions' really gone? What a preposterous last sentence, for while I continue to write, their continued existence must be supposed. A long way from the enigmatic smile of Kasyapa I am still at work taking bearings and keeping my humble Ship's Log up to date. Poetry creates these clear imperatives – not thinking so loud, letting the heartbeats break the codes embedded in the vowels. And then, in daily life, others created out of the tensions of events; to be the equal of reality you must learn how to ignore it without danger!

So the search must go on, poem by poem, until one strikes the obvious disengagement strategy so as to enter the stream of Heraclitean time at last. Great truths, one discovers, are not necessarily Facts – Facts are dreams.

NOTES

1   Chang, Jolan, *The Tao of Love and Sex*, Wildwood House, London, 1977.
2   Needham, Joseph, *Science and Civilization in China*, Cambridge University Press, 6 vols.
3   Yes, absurd, for had I strayed into a Tantric temple and seen wall-decorations involving jovial acts of cannibalism, ghosts drinking blood from skulls, and tearing human bodies limb from limb to eat them, I might easily have had a shock in the opposite sense.
4   The full address of the Chateau De Plaige is: Kagu-Ling, College Monastique, Chateau de Plaige France 71320.